THE
TREATY

THE
TREATY

Every New Zealander's Guide to the Treaty of Waitangi

MARCIA STENSON

RANDOM HOUSE
NEW ZEALAND

National Library of New Zealand Cataloguing-in-Publication Data
Stenson, Marcia.
The Treaty : Every New Zealander's Guide to the Treaty of
Waitangi / Marcia Stenson.
Includes bibliographical references.
ISBN 1-86941-631-7
1. Treaty of Waitangi (1840) 2. Sovereignty—Moral and ethical
aspects—New Zealand. 2. Maori (New Zealand people)—
Government relations. 3. Maori (New Zealand people)—Politics
and government. 4. Maori (New Zealand people)—Legal status,
laws, etc. 5. Maori (New Zealand people)—Land tenure. 5. New
Zealand—History. I. Title.
323.1199442—dc 22

A RANDOM HOUSE BOOK
published by
Random House New Zealand
18 Poland Road, Glenfield, Auckland, New Zealand
www.randomhouse.co.nz

First published 2004

© 2004 text Marcia Stenson; illustrations as credited on p 156

The moral rights of the author have been asserted

ISBN 1 86941 631 7

Design: Graeme Leather
Cover design: Dexter Fry
Cover photograph: Photobank
Printed in Australia by Griffin Press

Contents

Acknowledgements   6
Introduction   7

1   The Treaty of Waitangi   11

2   The Principles of the Treaty of Waitangi   20

3   Before the Treaty   29

4   The Signing of the Treaty of Waitangi   43

5   After the Treaty and up to 1975   50

6   The Crucial Issue of Land   66

7   The Waitangi Tribunal 1975   81

8   Some Examples of Tribunal Claims   94

9   Fisheries and the Treaty   111

10   The Treaty, the Lawyers and the Politicians   122

11   Seabed and Foreshore   131

12   Some Common Questions   145

Further Reading   153
Illustration Credits   156

Acknowledgements

My thanks go to all those who have helped me put this book together. My special thanks go to my schoolmates at Tokomaru Bay Maori District High School, whose photo is below.

The third form at Tokomaru Bay Maori District High School 1953. The author is in the front row, third from the right.

Introduction

In the more than 160 years since the Treaty was signed at Waitangi on 6 February 1840, it has had a chequered history. Against a background of enormous social and political change, it was ignored and relegated to the status of a quaint historical document by one group of signatories; while the other signatories and their descendants tried in vain to remind the others of the promises and values the Treaty contained. While Pakeha New Zealand did its best to ignore the Treaty, Maori New Zealand kept it always in sight.

In the latter part of the twentieth century a number of factors drove all New Zealanders to take another look at their founding document, to consider more seriously the claims of those who said they had been cheated, who were insisting that the Treaty be validated, be made part of the law of the land so that its promises could be realised.

Since then we have been arguing extensively, publishing endlessly, demonstrating occasionally. The debates have waxed and waned; everyone has an opinion that everyone else should be listening to. New issues have engulfed us — in part because a bigger population and higher expectations have put more pressure on our natural resources. In the 1980s one of the issues was who had the right to fish and where; at other times it was how we should handle Waitangi Day celebrations and what they really meant. In 2003 and 2004 the issue keeping us awake at night has been who could or should own parts of the seabed and foreshore.

The emphasis has moved from the actual words of the Treaty itself to the underlying principles. We inherited democracy from the Greeks but modified it to include a wider range of people. The American Constitution, too, had to be amended to include the large proportion of its population who were slaves and women. In the same way, it is unrealistic to expect a document rattled up in a hurry nearly 170 years ago to fit neatly into the 21st century. The process of defining and realising the principles will be a long one — especially as we realise the system of government and law inherited from Britain may not be an exact fit for a Pacific nation in the 21st century. We are beginning to realise that the Treaty will be an important part of our future as well as of our past and present.

Many of us grew up in a time when the Treaty was just a dusty parchment on the classroom wall. Some have disliked the uncertainty; have longed for it all to be over, finished, forgotten so we can 'get on with our lives', as they say. I am not one of them. I think that taking the Treaty, or in other words the Maori–Pakeha relationship, out of the closet where it was stuck for many a long year, giving it a jolly good shake, dusting it off and deciding where we go from here, was a very healthy thing for a society to do. To debate the issues, to decide what the Treaty really means today, to disagree and work out positive compromises is a characteristic of a democratic, forward-looking nation. I am proud to participate in the process.

My own background has been similar to that of many New Zealanders. I lived in rural areas, side by side with Maori communities, went to schools of predominantly Maori pupils, usually in a classroom with a portrait of Lieutenant Te Moananui-a-Kiwa Ngarimu, the first Maori awarded the Victoria Cross, on the wall behind me. Not until I studied history, taught history, wrote about New Zealand's past, did I feel I had a better understanding of the society I had grown up in.

This book is my chance to contribute to the debate. Much has been written about the Treaty already, but often by specialists in law, history, politics or race relations. I have tried to present the key information directly and simply, in order to make the main issues accessible. My hope is that you, the reader, can build on this framework to decide for yourself how we should move in the future.

Marcia Stenson

Chapter 1

The Treaty of Waitangi

The Treaty itself

There are two texts. They are not a direct translation of each other. This is the text signed by 43 northern chiefs at Waitangi on 6 February 1840:

Te Tiriti o Waitangi

Ko Wikitoria te Kuini o Ingarani i tana mahara atawai ki nga Rangatira me nga Hapu o Nu Tirani i tana hiahia hoki kia tohungia ki a ratou o ratou rangatiratanga me to ratou wenua, a kia mau tonu hoki te Rongo ki a ratou me te Atanoho hoki kua wakaaro ia he mea tika kia tukua mai tetahi Rangatira — hei kai wakarite ki nga Tangata maori o Nu Tirani — kia wakaaetia e nga Rangatira maori te Kawanatanga o te Kuini ki nga wahikatoa o te wenua nei me nga motu — na te mea hoki he tokomaha ke nga tangata o tonu Iwi Kua noho ki tenei wenua, a e haere mai nei.

Na ko te Kuini e hiahia ana kia wakaritea te Kawanatanga kia kaua ai nga kino e puta mai ki te tangata maori ki te Pakeha e noho ture kore ana.

Na kua pai te Kuini kia tukua a hau a Wiremu Hopihona he Kapitana i te Roiara Nawi hei Kawana mo nga wahi katoa o Nu Tirani e tukua aianei amua atu ki te Kuini, e mea atu ana ia ki nga

Rangatira o te wakaminenga o nga hapu o Nu Tirani me era Rangatira atu enei ture ka korerotia nei.

Ko te tuatahi

Ko nga Rangatira o te wakaminenga me nga Rangatira katoa hoki ki hai i uru ki taua wakaminenga ka tuku rawa atu ki te Kuini o Ingarani ake tonu atu — te Kawanatanga katoa o o ratou wenua.

Ko te tuarua

Ko te Kuini o Ingarani ka wakarite ka wakaae ki nga Rangatira ki nga hapu — ki nga tangata katoa o Nu Tirani te tino rangatiratanga o o ratou wenua o ratou kainga me o ratou Taonga katoa. Otiia ko nga Rangatira o te wakaminenga me nga Rangatira katoa atu ka tuku ki te Kuini te hokonga o era wahi wenua e pai ai te tangata nona te wenua — ki te ritenga o te utu e wakaritea ai e ratou ko te kai hoko e meatia nei e te Kuini hei kai hoko mona.

Ko te tuatoru

Hei wakaritenga mai hoki tenei mo te wakaaetanga ki te Kawanatanga o te Kuini — Ka tiakina e te Kuini o Ingarani nga tangata maori katoa o Nu Tirani ka tukua ki a ratou nga tikanga katoa rite tahi ki ana mea ki nga tangata o Ingarani.

[signed] W. Hobson Consul & Lieutenant Governor

Na ko matou ko nga Rangatira o te Wakaminenga o nga hapu o Nu Tirani ka huihui nei ki Waitangi ko matou hoki ko nga Rangatira o Nu Tirani ka kite nei i te ritenga o enei kupu. Ka tangohia ka wakaaetia katoatia e matou, koia ka tohungia ai o matou ingoa o matou tohu.

Ka meatia tenei ki Waitangi i te ono o nga ra o Pepueri i e tau kotahi mano, e waru rau e wa te kau o to tatou Ariki.

Then followed the heading :

Ko nga Rangatira o te Wakaminenga

followed by the names of the chiefs.

What does it mean?

Look for the following newly invented expressions:

　　Kuini o Ingarani = Queen of England

　　Kawanatanga = sovereignty

　　Nu Tirani = New Zealand

　　Wiremu Hopihona = William Hobson

　　Kapitana i te Roiara Nawi = Captain of the Royal Navy

Need some help understanding the crucial second article (Ko te tuarua)? Look out for these words:

　　te tino rangatiratanga = chieftainship

　　o ratou wenua = your lands

　　o ratou kainga = your village settlements

　　o ratou Taonga = your most precious possessions

This next text was the one signed at the Waikato Heads and Manakau by 39 chiefs in March/April 1840:

The Treaty of Waitangi

Her Majesty Victoria Queen of the United Kingdom of Great Britain and Ireland regarding with Her Royal Favor the Native Chiefs and Tribes of New Zealand and anxious to protect their just Rights and Property and to secure to them the enjoyment of Peace and Good Order has deemed it necessary in consequence of the great number of Her Majesty's Subjects who have already settled in New Zealand and the rapid extension of Emigration both from Europe and Australia which is still in progress to constitute and appoint a functionary properly authorised to treat with the Aborigines of New Zealand for the recognition of Her Majesty's sovereign authority over the whole or any part of those islands — Her Majesty therefore being desirous to establish a settled form of Civil Government with a view to avert the evil consequences which must result from the absence of the necessary Laws and Institutions alike to the native population and to Her subjects has been graciously pleased to empower and to authorise me William Hobson a Captain in Her Majesty's Royal Navy Consul and Lieutenant Governor of such parts of New Zealand as may be or hereafter shall be ceded to Her Majesty to invite the confederated and independent Chiefs of New Zealand to concur in the following Articles and Conditions.

Article the first

The Chiefs of the Confederation of the United Tribes of New Zealand and the separate and independent Chiefs who have not become members of the Confederation cede to Her Majesty the Queen of England absolutely and without reservation all the rights and powers of Sovereignty which the said Confederation or Individual Chiefs respectively exercise or possess, or may be supposed to exercise or possess over their respective Territories as the sole sovereigns thereof.

Article the second
Her Majesty the Queen of England confirms and guarantees to the Chiefs and Tribes of New Zealand and to the respective families and individuals thereof the full exclusive and undisturbed possession of their Lands and Estates Forests Fisheries and other properties which they may collectively or individually possess so long as it is their wish and desire to retain the same in their possession: but the Chiefs of the United Tribes and the individual Chiefs yield to Her Majesty the exclusive right of Preemption over such lands as the proprietors thereof may be disposed to alienate at such prices as may be agreed upon between the respective Proprietors and persons appointed by Her Majesty to treat with them in that behalf.

Article the third
In consideration thereof Her Majesty the Queen of England extends to the Natives of New Zealand Her royal protection and imparts to them all the Rights and Privileges of British Subjects.

[signed] W. Hobson Lieutenant Governor

Now therefore We the Chiefs of the Confederation of the United Tribes of New Zealand being assembled in Congress at Victoria in Waitangi and We the Separate and Independent Chiefs of New Zealand claiming authority over the Tribes and Territories which are specified after our respective names, having been made fully to understand the Provisions of the foregoing Treaty, accept and enter into the same in the full spirit and meaning thereof in witness of which we have attached our signatures or marks at the places and the dates respectively specified.

Done at Waitangi this Sixth day of February in the year of Our Lord one thousand eight hundred and forty.

About the Treaty

This agreement between the British Crown and the Maori people was signed on the sixth of February 1840 by 43 Northland chiefs and Lieutenant Governor Hobson. He was the official representative of Queen Victoria, the young woman reigning over the British Empire. It had been debated extensively the previous day, the fifth of February, at Waitangi. Over the following eight months the originals and copies were taken by Captain Hobson around Maori communities, mostly in coastal locations. After much discussion and debate, over 500 chiefs, including six women, signed. Most of them used a cross or moko (a signature tattoo). The few who signed their names (less than 15 percent), wrote in a wobbly hand. The Maori text has most of the signatures. The English text has an extra 39 Maori signatures. Today, both originals and copies are in the National Archives in Wellington.

The Maori chiefs signed willingly. Maori communities were full of battle-hardened, armed warriors not at all intimidated by Hobson and his armed escort of four troopers and a sergeant. Anyway, Maori chiefs were confident in their power. In 1840, New Zealand was a Maori world, where Pakeha were outnumbered by at least 50 to one.

The English version (when copies were made, slight differences happened so if you want to be nit-picky there were about five English versions) was the 'official' version for many years. However, it is the Maori version that has been seen as more important in recent times. It was the one most Maori chiefs signed. In international law — and New Zealand prides itself on following international rules — the version that matters is the one that was understood by the indigenous people.

What were the main points of the Treaty?

There were three main points.

1 The first declared that the Chiefs of New Zealand would hand over to the Queen of England absolutely and without reservation, all the rights and powers of sovereignty . . . over their territories. In the Maori version the word for sovereignty was kawanatanga.

What does it mean?

Sovereignty was a difficult concept to translate into Maori. Kawanatanga or governorship was an invented word, a transliteration of the English word 'governor'. The missionaries had used it for governors like Pontius Pilate in the Bible or governors of New South Wales. So, for those who had contact with missionaries, it was a familiar term for a powerful authority. Some commentators have said that mana would have been more accurate and that Reverend Henry Williams, in translating the document into Maori, deliberately blurred the meaning. Certainly, in 1835, James Busby had preferred mana to express the full power of the chiefs in the land. However, in 1985, the Waitangi Tribunal decided that Kawanatanga was appropriate, deliberately pragmatic, and not designed to remove mana.

---

2 In the second article, the Queen guaranteed to the chiefs, their tribes and families the full and exclusive possession of their Lands and Estates Forests Fisheries and other properties as long as they wanted to keep them. In the Maori version, rangatiratanga was to stay with the chiefs. This has been interpreted as *implying a shared authority, even a guarantee of Maori sovereignty*. The English version did not

mention chieftainship. Also in the Maori version, possessions were not spelt out so fully; instead the phrase ratou taonga katoa (all your precious treasures) was used. As well, the Queen and her representatives would have the first option on buying Maori land.

What does it mean?

The phrase finally chosen by Busby and Williams for the Maori version was te tino rangatiratanga, the fullness or essence of chieftainship. The word rangatira (chief) was widely used and universally adopted by Europeans for the Maori leaders they met in many different circumstances. It was the term used for heads of whanau (extended families) and of hapu (the kin groups or functioning tribes).

What does it mean?

Busby wrote the clause about chieftainship over land, villages and all valued treasures to be retained by Maori. Taonga or 'Treasures' was spelt out in the English version to include all the resources of the land, including forests and fisheries. A recent interpretation has been to include te reo, the Maori language, as one of the Taonga — the rationale for support for Maori TV.

---

3 The third article extended the Queen's protection over Maori. They were to enjoy all the rights and privileges of British subjects. The emphasis later was to be on the special relationship between the monarch and Maori.

The Treaty today

The Treaty is very important in New Zealand's legal framework, although it is not directly enforceable in New Zealand courts. However, specific legislation does provide for the Principles of the Treaty to be considered, or that certain provisions should be interpreted in accordance with the Principles.

Key Points

- There were several versions of the Treaty.
- The Maori one was signed by most of the chiefs and is the version they understood.
- The English version gave the Crown more and Maori less.
- References to the Principles of the Treaty are included in many of our laws.

Further Reading

The Treaty of Waitangi by Claudia Orange

Making Peoples: A History of the New Zealanders from Polynesian settlement to the end of the Nineteenth Century by James Belich

Government website: www.treatyofwaitangi.govt.nz

Chapter 2

The Principles of the Treaty of Waitangi

We have reinterpreted the Treaty several times in our history and we may do so again. Getting to grips with an agreement made over 160 years ago is hard enough, but when that agreement is in two languages, things get really tricky. Views are deeply divided even between Pakeha, not just between Maori and Pakeha. Looking for a definite answer is like seeking to find the correct meaning of the Bible or the Koran. The different groups are absolutely sure that theirs is the correct version.

People have increasingly turned to the spirit of the Treaty as expressed in its principles. It has been viewed as a document, historically valid but needing a contemporary interpretation. The Principles of the Treaty of Waitangi, a term seldom used before the 1980s, is now a very familiar phrase. A number of Acts of Parliament require acknowledgement of these principles. But those seeking definitive answers are likely to be disappointed for there is no general agreement on exactly what these principles are. As new principles emerge and old ones are modified, we will have to be sure to check back with the original document to make sure that the principles haven't replaced the Treaty itself.

The Treaty of Waitangi Act 1975, which established the Waitangi Tribunal, stressed the practical application of the principles. The Tribunal is charged with giving weight to both

Maori and English versions of the Treaty. It treats the Treaty as a living force, a basic constitutional document which provides direction for future growth and development. In the Privy Council (1994) explanation, the difference between the Treaty's actual words and the Treaty principles was that the principles are the *underlying mutual obligations and responsibilities* which the Treaty places on the parties. They reflect the intent of the Treaty as a whole.

Different versions of the principles of the Treaty of Waitangi

The Court of Appeal's version 1987

The Court of Appeal considered the Principles of the Treaty to be the same today as they were when it was signed in 1840. It is the circumstances to which those principles are to apply that have changed greatly.

As defined by the Court of Appeal in *New Zealand Maori Council and Graham Stanley Latimer v. the Attorney General and others,* June 1987:

> The Treaty provides for the acquisition of sovereignty in exchange for the protection of rangatiratanga

Mr Justice Cooke stated that the basic terms of the Treaty bargain are partly conflicting. The Queen to govern, Maori to be her subjects — in return their chieftainships and possessions to be protected, but sales of land to the Crown could be negotiated. The Treaty has to be seen as an embryo rather than a fully developed and integrated set of ideas.

> The Treaty requires a partnership and the duty to act reasonably and in good faith

Mr Justice Cooke said that the principles require Pakeha and

Maori Treaty partners to act towards each other reasonably and with utmost good faith.

> The Treaty provides for the freedom of the Crown to govern

The parties owe each other co-operation.

> The Treaty bestows on the Crown a duty of active protection of Maori people in the use of their lands and waters to the fullest extent practicable
> The Crown has a duty to remedy past breaches of the Treaty
> The Treaty provides for Maori to retain chieftainship (rangatiratanga) over their resources and taonga and to have all the rights and privileges of citizenship
> The Treaty bestows on Maori a duty of reasonable co-operation

The judge added that this was not a one-sided arrangement but involved a duty for the Crown to consult.

The Court of Appeal saw the concept of partnership as the Treaty's most important contribution. Partnership, in the view of the Court, suggests obligations on both parties, Maori and Pakeha. It recognises separate identity and implies a pattern of mutual obligation. It suggests sharing power; it is flexible. It is an interpretation to fit changing circumstances. What partnership means today is very different from what it meant in 1840. But the Court did not spell out exactly what the partnership should be. Is it to be 50/50 or 80/20 or what?

The Government's version

The Labour Government defined the principles in 1989. These were modified in 1990 by the following National Government.

Five Treaty principles

1 **Principle of Government (kawanatanga)** — more or less from the first article of the Treaty, establishes the Government's right to govern (fettered by the requirement to accord Maori interests specified in the second article an appropriate priority). National amended this after 1990 to indicate 'ought to govern for the common good'.

2 **Principle of Self-Management (rangatiratanga)** — confirms that iwi should have the right to organise as iwi and, under the law, control the resources they own. Amended by National after 1990 as self-management within the law.

3 **Principle of Equality** — all New Zealanders are equal before the law.

4 **Principle of Reasonable Co-operation between Iwi and Government**

5 **Principle of Redress** — the government is responsible for providing effective processes for resolution of grievances.

The New Zealand Maori Council's version

The New Zealand Maori Council was set up by the Government in 1962 to co-ordinate the District Maori Councils and to provide a voice for Maori. It identified ten principles which include:

- The duty to make good past breaches of the Treaty.
- The duty to return land for land.
- That the Maori way of life would be protected.
- The duty to consult Maori.
- That the parties would be of equal status.
- That priority would be given to Maori values with regard to taonga.

The Waitangi Tribunal's approach

The Waitangi Tribunal was set up in 1975 to hear Maori grievances against the Crown. It uses a case-by-case approach in its analysis, and states only those principles relevant to the case before it. In the Muriwhenua Land Report the Tribunal saw the principles as enlarging the terms, allowing the Treaty to be applied in situations not foreseen or discussed when it was signed. The principles overlap; they are not separate from each other like a checklist. From a number of Tribunal decisions a series of common core principles can be found, including:

1. The essential bargain was the exchange of the right to make laws for the obligation to protect Maori interests.

   Kawanatanga. We think this is something less than the sovereignty (or absolute authority) ceded in the English text. As used in the Treaty it means the authority to make laws for the order and security of the country but subject to an undertaking to protect particular Maori interest.
   [Manukau Report of the Waitangi Tribunal, 1985, p 90]

2. The Treaty implies a partnership, with mutual obligations to act towards each other in good faith.

   Maori must recognise those things that reasonably go with good governance just as the Crown must recognise those things that reasonably go with being Maori.
   [Te Whanau o Waipareira Report of the Waitangi Tribunal, 1998, p 29]

3. The Treaty is able to be adapted to meet new situations.

   We consider that the Treaty is capable of a measure of adaptation to meet new and changing circumstances provided there is a measure of consent and adherence to its broad principles.
   [Motunui Report of the Waitangi Tribunal, 1983, p 61]

4 Compromise is needed on both sides, so the needs of both Maori and Pakeha can be met.

It is not consistent with the Treaty's spirit that the resolution of an unfair situation for one party creates an unfair situation for another.

[Report on the Waiheke Island Claim, 1989, p 41]

5 The principle of redress for Treaty breaches flows from the Crown's duty to act reasonably and in good faith as a Treaty partner.

. . . the redress of Treaty grievances is necessary to restore the honour and integrity of the Crown and the mana and status of Maori.

[The Tarawera Forest Report, 2003, p 29]

The Office of Treaty Settlements spells out the partnership

The Office of Treaty Settlements was set up by the Government in 1995 to oversee settlements and when necessary negotiate with claimants. A 1999 publication sees the partnership, as defined by the Court of Appeal, as reflecting the following four principles:

1 **Fiduciary duty** — the relationship between the Treaty partners creates responsibilities like those of a trustee. The Crown has a duty to actively protect Maori interests.

2 **Full spirit of co-operation** — each party is to act reasonably and in good faith towards one another.

3 **The honour of the Crown** — the Treaty is a positive force in the life of the country and therefore in the government of the country.

4. **Fair and reasonable redress** — the Crown should not impede its capacity to give fair and reasonable redress.

How to interpret the Treaty today

The modern interpretation of the Treaty of Waitangi assumes all Maori have accepted sovereignty of the Crown and therefore the sovereignty of the New Zealand Parliament and its laws. Some iwi didn't sign the Treaty, and those signing got a very different government from the one they were probably expecting. The Court of Appeal has made it clear that the Treaty implies full acceptance of the sovereignty of Parliament and its laws.

There would be very few Maori who don't accept British sovereignty. Most concentrate instead on its failure to keep its part of the bargain, a failure to recognise Maori property rights. In the words of Sir Tipene ORegan:

> Right, you've got your sovereignty. You also guaranteed us two other articles and you haven't delivered on them. To some extent you delivered on one — the one about citizenship — but on the other you put down the deposit and drove the car out of the yard. You failed the contract but we have to watch you drive that car up and down the road every day — and it hurts!
>
> [from *Maori, Pakeha and Democracy* by Richard Mulgan, OUP, 1989, p 105]

No one is trying to return to 1840. The Tribunal does not ask for complete restitution of lands or fisheries. With the Manukau claim, for example, the Tribunal did not agree that fishing rights in the whole harbour should be given to Maori tribes, so excluding Pakeha fishing.

Nor does it try to assess the present value of the land. For example, the claim involving Orakei (prime real estate in Auckland), would have gone into many millions of dollars. The

Tribunal tries to assess the amount needed to provide for present and future needs of the tribe. It makes no sense for the resolution of one injustice to create another.

The Principles of the Treaty are not an enforcement of agreements made in 1840 or even a righting of wrongs done since then. They are a commitment to *justice for all* in the present and the future.

The Principles cannot be an exact translation of any version of the Treaty because New Zealand is very different now from the situation in 1840. Interpreting rather than translating the Treaty makes more sense. Take one instance from the Maori version, the word taonga. The preservation of language and culture was not specified in the Maori version. Taonga has since been interpreted by both Maori and Pakeha (after some legal battles) to mean anything Maori valued highly even if it was not an issue at the time.

The Principles now tell us more about the values of present-day society than the intentions of those who actually framed and signed it. The Treaty and the Principles remind us all as New Zealanders that our history and traditions are built on guarantees made to safeguard Maori interests and identity in return for acceptance of settlers and allegiance to the Crown.

Key Points

- There are several different versions of the Principles of the Treaty.
- The Principles are a commitment to justice for all in the present and the future.
- The Treaty is not just about righting past wrongs, it is about future lines of development.

Further Reading

Maori, Pakeha and Democracy by Richard Mulgan

The Treaty Now by William Renwick

Trick or Treaty? by Douglas Graham

Te Mana, Te Kawanatanga: the Politics of Maori Self-Determination by Mason Durie

Chapter 3

Before the Treaty

A Maori world

Some time between AD 250 and AD 1150, expert Polynesian long-distance sailors, deliberately looking for land, arrived in New Zealand. With a founding population of at least 70 women, there must have been several canoes arriving at roughly the same time.

The new land, vast by comparison with a Pacific island or atoll, must at first have appeared to contain boundless supplies of food. The moa was butchered in big numbers and over-fishing led to a decline in snapper, seal and sea lion harvests. Snapper, for example, was fished to extinction in the South Island. In the north the average size of snapper declined rapidly. As protein supplies slumped there were times of food shortage and starvation. Archaeologists have found weakened human skeletons with teeth completely ground down by a fibrous diet. The population fluctuated rather than increased steadily. Life could be very hard.

To generate more bracken growth the bush was fired, particularly in the South Island. Probably 40 percent of the original forest cover was deliberately or accidentally destroyed. At least 20 species of birds were hunted to extinction. The kiore and Polynesian dog also contributed to the extinction of many birds and insects.

The archaeological record shows clearly that the early Maori experience in New Zealand was remarkably similar to that of the Pakeha. Both squandered resources when they first arrived. The notion of living in harmony with nature in a spiritual relationship came later as they learnt to balance their needs, and became more conservation-conscious and respectful of the environment.

What does it mean?

Maori meant 'normal' or 'usual'. The original inhabitants did not call themselves Maori. They were Nga Puhi, Ngati Maniapoto or Tuhoe or any of 40 or more tribes. The idea of a nation or national identity did not exist. One's identity came from the hapu, the iwi and the environment. So members of Ngati Porou, the tribe of the North Island's East Coast, took their identity from Ngati Porou ancestors, the Waiapu River and the mountain Hikurangi. Ngati Tuwharetoa, on the other hand, identified with Tongariro Mountain, Lake Taupo and the ancestor Te Heuheu. It was not until pale-skinned strangers arrived that Maori first used the word to describe themselves.

The Maori social system was organised around kinship and the importance of mana, tapu and utu. Knowledge was transmitted orally. The skills of debate were important and highly respected. A skilled orator was a leader of men. Fighting skill and strength were important but had to be combined with other qualities.

What does it mean?

Mana means status or authority, gained by providing for the people, not oneself. It was the main motivating factor in Maori society. Utu refers to keeping life in balance by reciprocal exchanges in relationships between individuals, groups and ancestors. Tapu means sacred or under restriction. These values remain strong today.

Relationship with the land

Maori saw themselves as users of the land, and even felt they belonged to the land rather than that the land belonged to them. Maori contracts were all about defining relationships between people. There was no Maori word for 'sale'.

The kin group shared amongst themselves the resources of the land, the inland waters, the seas, the forests, and the gardens. E. T. Durie, a Chief Judge of the Maori Land Court, described Maori tenure as ancestral trust estate, vested in hapu but with use rights distributed among ancestral descendants and incorporated outsiders who used them. Use rights were transferable within families but not outside the group, unless the general group gave permission.

Customary Maori title included:

- **Take tipu or take tupuna** — ancestral land passed down according to custom.

- **Take raupatu** — land taken by conquest. But conquest without occupation did not give the conqueror a right to those lands.

- **Take tuku** — land gifted, perhaps from a dying chief in order to strengthen relationships with a neighbouring tribe. The land had to be occupied and used by the recipient.

- **Take taunaha** — land which had been unoccupied with no known claimants. The discoverer had to occupy it and use it to keep it.

Use rights depended on the user occupying the land, being there continually, and being able to defend it. Te ahi ka was the right of occupation. It was generally accepted that the fires of occupation had gone out after three generations or more. A defeated tribe could still lay claim to their land if survivors were still there, even if they were slaves or vassals. But the best guarantee of a right to the land was having the military strength to defend it.

Each new season the hapu moved to the area where they had the rights to gather or harvest that season's fish, berries, birds, shellfish or other resources, or to grow kumara. The community understood perfectly well who had a right to what. Later, transferring this crazy patchwork to an English type of individual title was very difficult.

Sometimes use rights began in a very complicated way. Here is an example found by Angela Ballara in the records of the Land Court, showing how land transactions even as late as 1865 were more about defining relationships between people than transferring property. During a period of warfare and social disruption that affected the hapu of Te Aitanga-a-Mahaki, the chief Te Iho-o-te-rangi was living with his family and followers as refugees. They were cut off from their usual resources:

> Te Iho o te rangi on one occasion packed up his bird snares and carried them on his back and he was seen going along in the bush carrying his snares on his back and looking about from tree to tree by Whatungarongaro . . . Now Whatungarongaro had been there before and asked for a tree and one had been given to him by Takuha, and Whatungarongaro seeing the old man going about with his snares took pity on him and told him to put the snares on the tree given him by Takuha. When Takuha heard this he came and gave Te Iho o te rangi the five or six trees at this bend [of the Waihora River] and that became his property.
> [Ballara, p195]

Eventually, in Land Court days, Ngati Matepu, the descendants of Te Iho-o-te-rangi, were able to claim these few acres of land.

A major hapu was unlikely to have its land in one block. There were few fixed borders or frontiers. It was more important to make sure others recognised your rights. Though there were disputes over ownership, there was no unclaimed land. There was a name for every feature of the land, for every fishing ground, reef and prominent ledge at sea. As a Muriwhenua submission reported:

> Travellers in their own countryside could name its features minutely — rocks, caves, fishing grounds, points, streams, eeling pools, patches of bush, cultivations, swamps, rat-runs, trees, ridges, hills and mountains, even clumps of grass — every smallest feature had its name which evoked the quality of that unique place, and nga tupuna, the ancestors who had named it or passed that way.
> [Muriwhenua Land Report 1997, pp 18–19]

Not everything was communally owned. There were family and individual canoes and eel traps for instance. However, land was always held by and for the hapu. An individual's right to use the land came from his or her membership of the hapu.

European land values
In European tradition, ownership is established by a written deed of sale, rather than by use. Owning the title deeds is more important than being a long-standing occupier. The value of the land has little to do with spiritual or cultural values and everything to do with market potential. However, Pakeha too can develop a spiritual connection with the land, over time.

Social relationships

The hapu was the primary unit of Maori society. It was more important in everyday life than the iwi. The chief and the hapu needed each other for protection and support, though the chief's authority could be challenged or rejected by the hapu. The mana of the chief was all-important. He did not own everything, but while he was accepted as the proper bearer of mana he (who could occasionally be she) had the right to make decisions about the land and the various hapu living under his mana or authority.

What does it mean?

Hapu is an extended family or families. Iwi was originally the loose confederation of hapu who shared a common ancestor. Today, iwi is used for the larger tribal unit, usually the negotiating agent with the Crown, but the hapu is still more relevant to many Maori.

Even within the iwi network, each hapu strove to maintain its independence. When war began, each hapu made its own battle decisions under its own chiefs. The paramount chief, or ariki, did not rule but had the responsibility of expressing the wish of the whole tribe.

Which tribes were where

Northland

At the end of the 18th century in Northland there were three main groups of tribes. North of the Bay of Islands five tribes were known as the Muriwhenua (Ngati Kahu, Ngati Kuri, Ngai Takoto, Aupouri and Rarawa). The tribes of central Northland (such as Ngati Pou, Ngati Rehia and Ngare Raumati) in the 19th

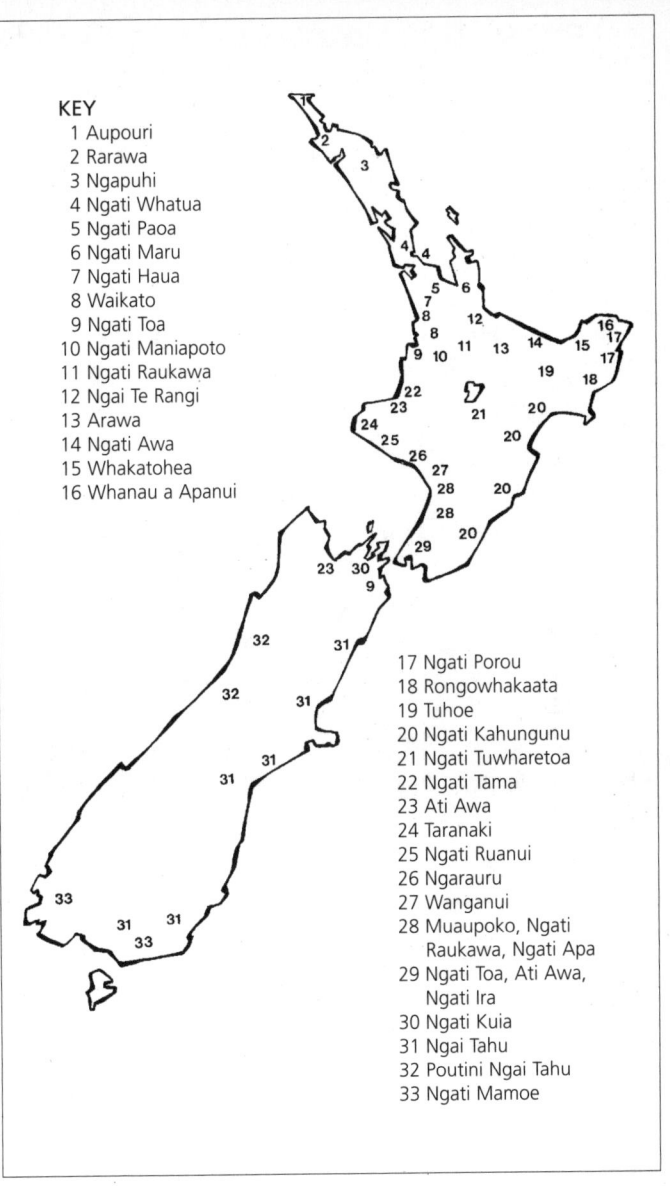

KEY
1 Aupouri
2 Rarawa
3 Ngapuhi
4 Ngati Whatua
5 Ngati Paoa
6 Ngati Maru
7 Ngati Haua
8 Waikato
9 Ngati Toa
10 Ngati Maniapoto
11 Ngati Raukawa
12 Ngai Te Rangi
13 Arawa
14 Ngati Awa
15 Whakatohea
16 Whanau a Apanui

17 Ngati Porou
18 Rongowhakaata
19 Tuhoe
20 Ngati Kahungunu
21 Ngati Tuwharetoa
22 Ngati Tama
23 Ati Awa
24 Taranaki
25 Ngati Ruanui
26 Ngarauru
27 Wanganui
28 Muaupoko, Ngati Raukawa, Ngati Apa
29 Ngati Toa, Ati Awa, Ngati Ira
30 Ngati Kuia
31 Ngai Tahu
32 Poutini Ngai Tahu
33 Ngati Mamoe

Traditional tribal locations, c. 1870

BEFORE THE TREATY 35

century came to form one kin zone, Nga Puhi. Further south but still in Northland were Ngati Whatua and Ngati Paoa. They both had kin ties with the tribes of the Coromandel and the East Coast.

Tainui

Tainui settled at Kawhia in the 15th century and expanded into the interior. There were three distinct groupings: Ngati Paoa of Hauraki with its allies, Ngati Maru, Ngati Tamatera and Ngati Whanaunga who controlled Coromandel and the Auckland isthmus; the Waikato group of Ngati Maniapoto, Ngati Haua and others; and further south were Ngati Raukawa and Ngati Toa.

Bay of Plenty

These tribes, linked to the Arawa canoe, had spread inland from Maketu. They included Ngai Te Rangi and Ngati Ranginui. In the Rotorua–Taupo area were Ngati Tuwharetoa, who had strong links with Waikato and Bay of Plenty.

East Coast

Those tribes with links to the Mataatua canoe included the Tuhoe in the Urewera, Ngati Awa and Whakatohea. Ngati Porou were further south.

Taranaki–Whanganui

Ties with the Aotea or Aotearoa canoe linked Te Ati Awa with three other North Taranaki tribes: Ngati Mutunga, Ngati Tama and Ngati Maru. In South Taranaki were Taranaki, Ngati Ruanui and Nga Rauru. Along the river were the large Whanganui tribes, at least a hundred hapu with kin ties north and south. The Whanganui River was a busy trading thoroughfare, the lifeline between northern New Zealand and the south.

North and south of Cook Strait

Intermarriage and interaction took place on both sides of the strait. It presented no problem to competent sailors. About 600 hapu and 30 hapu groups stretched from northern Hawke's Bay through South Wairarapa to the tribes of Nelson–Marlborough and were linked to the Kurahaupo canoe. They were the southern branches of North Island groups. The tribe Abel Tasman got into strife with was Ngati Tumata, a powerful and self-confident tribe able to muster 300 warriors in two days but later pushed out of Marlborough.

Rest of the South Island

The Ngai Tahu dominated over hapu such as the Waitaha, Ngati Mamoe and Te Rapuwai.

Chatham Islands

These tribes had arrived in the Chathams probably around the 15th century — they were not a pre-Polynesian people. 'Moriori' refers to ancestral Maori who settled the Chatham Islands. They were in the forefront of Polynesian explorers but found themselves on an island with no canoe timber.

Key Points

- Maori land ownership was about relationships with people.
- Use rights, being able to defend the land and communal ownership characterised Maori ownership.
- Use rights formed a complex pattern.
- All the land was owned and named.

What does it mean?

Pakeha = the strangers. To begin with this meant all non-Maori. Today, however, it means non-Maori New Zealanders of European descent, so excluding people from the Pacific or Asia.

Arrival of the Pakeha

Abel Tasman (1642), James Cook (1769), de Surville (1769), Marion du Fresne (1772) and others all left accounts of their first meetings and interactions with Maori. These accounts often tell us more about European attitudes at that time than about Maori society. There were examples of violence: Abel Tasman lost several of his men and sailed off in a panic; Cook killed several Maori. These were exceptions, for most interaction was positive. Each needed something from the other. Maori showed great interest in industrial technology, converting goods like nails and axes to a multiplicity of purposes. Explorers needed good sheltered anchorages, access to fresh water, food, rest and recreation.

Language difficulties and understanding each other's cultural taboos caused problems, though. Pakeha explorers unwittingly broke social codes like heaving dead sailors overboard into local Maori fishing grounds. When they had died from scurvy, the corpses were not a pretty sight. Sometimes, like Marion du Fresne, they blundered into complex local battles for power and resources. Pakeha ships anchoring for several weeks often put impossible pressure on limited food supplies. Many Maori, too, paid a terrible price for contact with European diseases.

Whalers, sealers, traders and missionaries

The next wave of Pakeha were also passing through, looking for quick profits from natural resources like seals, whales, timber and flax. Whaling and sealing ships called for shelter and fresh supplies at the Bay of Islands. Early contacts with sealers were sometimes violent, but settled into peaceful mode by the 1830s. Sealers and shore whalers lived in semi-permanent, hybrid communities. They took long-term or short-term Maori wives. Some early settlers were escaped convicts or deserters from whaling ships. Those who stayed lived as Maori, becoming known as Pakeha Maori. By 1830 several trading stations were dealing in flax, timber and boat building, usually in exchange for guns and ammunition. Like the whaling stations, most were staffed and funded out of Sydney — New Zealand was part of Sydney's hinterland. After concerns about the rough, rude Europeans, their lawlessness and the impact on Maori, James Busby was appointed from New South Wales in 1833 as the first British Official.

Missionaries arrived after the Anglican Samuel Marsden set

'The Power of God's Word' (1856, artist unknown). Missionaries introduced both the written word and new concepts.

up the first mission in 1814. There were no converts at all until 1830. Hone Heke is said to have announced, while taking a mission station under his wing for trade reasons, that Christianity was not a religion suitable for a warrior. Wesleyans joined the Church Missionary Society in setting up missions, and in 1838, Bishop Pompallier began a successful Roman Catholic programme of conversion. By 1845 there were about 40 mission stations unevenly spread, some large, some small. They found it necessary, as did traders and ship captains, to have a close relationship with at least one Maori chief. They needed protection as well as supplies and workers. Maori chiefs were confident in their power.

It was a two-way interaction. Until the 1830s few Europeans were fluent in Maori. But many Maori were learning English and becoming familiar with the alien culture. Many shipped out as crew — not all voluntarily. Whaling captains replaced deserting seamen with reliable Maori hands. Many became pilots or harpooners. Others visited England as guests of missionaries or others. James Belich estimates that possibly a thousand Maori travelled overseas before 1840. Another thousand may have become informal partners/wives of European settlers, while yet another thousand worked closely with whalers and sealers. There were thousands of short-term sex contracts in the Bay of Islands, each, as Belich comments, 'a crash course in European customs and language'. [*Making Peoples*, p 145]

Tribes were keen to have their own 'Pakeha'. With a Pakeha, even of the missionary variety, came trade. Traders were amazed at how Maori used and adapted technology. One described a patu made by hours of work spent beating out an iron bar. At first it was large nails which were the most popular trade item, then iron tools in the 1790s and 1800s. After that, guns dominated. Muskets were necessary for survival in the bloody wars of retribution and revenge which occurred in the 1820s and '30s. Guns were stockpiled too as evidence of tribal wealth. But guns needed continuing supplies of ammunition. Only traders could supply the need, though there were some interesting experiments to produce local ammunition. Even the missionaries found themselves under pressure to repair the bloody weapons.

From the 1830s muskets were the basic currency of New Zealand commerce. Prices fell as the number of European settlers increased. This seemed a good reason for welcoming more settlers.

> **Musket currency**
>
> *1812 one gun = 8 large pigs and 150 baskets of potatoes*
>
> *1820s one gun =10 large pigs and 120 baskets of potatoes*
>
> *1830s one gun = 6 pigs*
>
> *Paying for one gun in dressed flax dropped from 1 ton per gun to 8 hundredweight (but this still involved 100 days' labour-intensive scraping of the fibre with a mussel shell — this was women's work). In the sex industry in the Bay of Islands, guns were also part of the price.* [Belich, p 152]

The widespread commercial dealings of the 1830s brought political change. As chiefs set the contract price terms for goods, flax, timber and the cost of the labour, more Maori were becoming exposed to prostitution, the abuse of alcohol and the trade in muskets. The missionaries became increasingly appalled by the abuses introduced by their compatriots.

Missions introduced the written word in the form of Bibles, stories, parables, texts and messages. New ideas entered an oral culture. By the later 1830s most Maori, whether in contact directly with missionaries or not, were in discussions about their religion. There were debates about beliefs and values in many Maori communities.

In welcoming settlers, Maori chiefs expected to be able to include Europeans within their communities under their own sets of rules. The absolute alienation of land was a new notion, but by the late 1830s many Maori were becoming aware of it. Particularly with northern and coastal tribes, these experiences of European attitudes to land ownership were fundamental to their discussions around the Treaty.

Key Points

- ❖ Colonisation was a two-way interaction between different cultures.
- ❖ Maori were eager to use the products and technology of industrial societies.
- ❖ Missions introduced new ideas through preaching and the written word.
- ❖ Maori were in control and expected to stay in control.

Further Reading

Two Worlds: First Meetings of Maori and Europeans 1642–1772 by Ann Salmond

The Quest For Origins: Who first discovered and settled New Zealand and the Pacific Islands? by Kerry Howe

Iwi: the Dynamics of Maori Tribal Organisation from c.1769–c.1945 by Angela Ballara

Making Peoples: A History of the New Zealanders from Polynesian settlement to the end of the Nineteenth Century by James Belich

Chapter 4

The Signing of the Treaty of Waitangi

On 6 February 1840 a large group of people gathered together at Waitangi in the Bay of Islands, New Zealand. It was, from all accounts, a stunning summer's day with a gentle breeze rippling over the sparkling waters of the bay. Maori war canoes sped across the water to land northern chiefs on the headland. Captain Hobson of the British Royal Navy, newly appointed Lieutenant Governor to New Zealand by Queen Victoria, had called them together to consider a document which was to become of crucial significance for New Zealand/Aotearoa. It was to be much discussed, constantly reinterpreted, and sometimes ignored or overlooked only to be revived. But there is no doubt that it was to be a document that does a great deal to define us as a nation. Truly, a founding document. What were the factors which had led to this vital meeting of the Maori chiefs and the spokesman for the British Queen and Parliament?

There had been an earlier attempt to establish a form of government in the north. In 1834, James Busby, the new British Resident, had presented the northern chiefs with three flags to choose from. After a speech by Busby on 20 March, one flag was chosen by the chiefs. They then declared themselves to be the United Tribes of New Zealand: *He Whakaputanga o te Rangatira o Nu Tireni*.

This declaration of independence had been Busby's idea, to cope with some specific difficulties. One was commercial. Ships built at the Horeke shipyard, in the Hokianga, had been seized at Port Jackson, Sydney's port, because they were not officially registered to any country. Busby's new flag would establish the ships' origins. This first New Zealand flag flew at Waitangi until 1840.

Busby also hoped to block a couple of potential European rivals. In the north there was a strange adventurer called de Thierry making wild claims, and further south there was a potential threat from the French Government. Neither of these were in fact very serious competitors to British power.

Busby was following instructions from his superior in New South Wales. He had been asked to establish a settled form of government and a system of laws. Busby took the Declaration of Independence seriously and sent it off to England with 34 signatories in November 1835. He collected more signatures, and by July 1839 had 52. Most were northern chiefs but he also managed to get the name of an important Waikato chief, Potatau Te Wherowhero.

Existing side by side

Potatau Te Wherowhero, a powerful Waikato chief, later refused to sign the Treaty. He was however, not strongly opposed to British sovereignty. He was prepared to let others of his tribe sign, and wrote letters to Queen Victoria about Governors Hobson and Grey commenting favourably on their work. Later, in 1858, he became the first Maori King under the title King Potatau I. At important occasions from 1857–58, the replica of the flag of the United Tribes of New Zealand was flown. He felt both authorities could exist side by side — the Queen over the Pakeha and the Maori King over the Maori.

The declaration asserted the rangatiratanga, or independent chieftainship of the land. For the first time Maori saw themselves as having a collective identity. The Declaration stated that the authority in the land (Ko te Kingitanga ko te mana i te whenua) resided in the chiefs in their collective capacity, and asked King William IV to be a parent to their infant state. The British Crown accepted this document in 1836. Some see this as creating a legal dilemma because the Crown was accepting both independence and a protectorate relationship. How it sits with the Treaty is also a question for discussion and debate. Can Britain recognise independence in 1836 and then sign a very different sort of treaty in 1840?

But this Declaration of Independence had little practical effect. Ordering the timber for a new Government House was about as far as Busby got in setting up a government. The New South Wales administration would not let him have the money to pay for building it. Meanwhile, some chiefs were becoming attracted to ideas of peace. Missionary teachings were beginning to have an impact. The notion of 'the law' — a missionary term to describe the idea of negotiated mediation when disputes began to spiral into violence — appealed to many Maori. Chiefs like Wiremu Tamihana Tarapipipi mediated in disputes. Busby also was finding that some of the northern chiefs were prepared to turn to him for help in arguments with Europeans, and even occasionally between Maori.

A different view
Te Waharoa Wiremu Tamihana Tarapipipi was a mission-educated, very influential Ngati Haua leader well known for his strong Christian beliefs and moderate views. Later he played a vital role in establishing the Kng movement, hoping to provide effective laws for his people.

The Treaty of Waitangi, a document written in semi-legal terms, nevertheless had a thousand years of literate history behind it. In an oral society quite different traditions had developed. In the discussions and deliberation on the marae, metaphors, parables and riddles demonstrated quite different ways of thinking and debate. But it was a society where a significant number of Maori adults were reading biblical texts in Maori and a few were even reading and writing letters in Maori. The Treaty was a series of propositions introduced into a world where there had, in many parts of the country, already been extensive discussions about the Pakeha. Should they be admitted into Maori communities and should they be protected?

In 1840 the balance of power still lay in Maori hands. Maori outnumbered Pakeha greatly. They had guns and knew how to use them. As the Wairau incident in 1843 was to show, they weren't inclined to just sit about when their rights were under threat. In most areas of the North Island they were very much in control. At the most, Hobson had an army of 12 New South Wales police troopers (often drunk) and a small civil service. British authority in New Zealand in 1840 was very dependent on Maori consent.

Why did Britain want a Treaty?

British motives were both pragmatic and idealistic. There was an ongoing threat of lawlessness for both Maori and law-abiding British settlers. There had been nasty incidents like one where the British Captain of the brig *Elizabeth* was involved in a murderous raid by Te Rauparaha on the South Island and then had skipped before he could be brought to justice.

Humanitarians, influenced also by the locally based missionaries, pressed for the establishment of a civil government to protect the rights of Maori exposed to the worst Pakeha vices. Missionaries and traders were not keen on having to put up with Maori 'protectors' either. They could survive only under the wing of a Maori chief but they resented it. There was also the issue of the boatloads of British settlers sent by Wakefield, due to arrive at Port Nicholson at any moment.

Hobson did not bring the Treaty from England. Both texts, Maori and English, were created at the Bay of Islands. The British Government had given him flexible instructions. He could obtain sovereignty over some or all of the country as he deemed appropriate. He was to make a treaty and to recognise Maori land-ownership, but he would not be given any military force. Hobson was therefore able to use the experience of older European residents like Reverend Henry Williams and James Busby. They at least had some clues about the relationship Maori had with the land.

Was the Treaty understood?

It is a recognised principle in international law that a treaty must be construed, not as lawyers and linguists understand it but as it was understood by those who actually signed it. Historian Judith Binney thinks that most who signed the Treaty did understand it. It was widely debated and not just at Waitangi. It was debated in the traditional, oral way. The propositions were queried, examined and some areas were specifically rejected.

Some chiefs were initially quite opposed, others were suspicious or questioned the translation, but after debate and discussion most signed. Hobson emphasised the protective role of the British Queen and her personal relationship with Maori. French Catholic priests, observing some of the proceedings and trying to be neutral, commented that the chiefs had no intention of giving up their territory or their sovereignty. There was no coercion, though. Accompanied by one sergeant and four armed troopers, Hobson was not in a position to use military force.

Why did the chiefs agree?

Over 500 chiefs signed the Treaty. Hone Heke, the powerful Nga Puhi chief, was the first of over 40 influential northern chiefs to sign. Many more than that number accepted official positions in the new state. There was no shortage of those wanting to sell land. Some chiefs did all three. Their reasons could often be found in local tribal politics and rivalry. Only important chiefs got to sign treaties and land deeds, to accept official positions. A Chief needed to get in quick before some rival stole his thunder. In some cases the material benefits were very tempting.

In August 1840, Te Puni of Te Ati Awa, who sold land in Wellington that was not his to sell, explained that he could not resist it when he saw so many muskets and blankets in front of him. But he had other reasons too. Both he and Te Wharepouri welcomed Pakeha settlement in Wellington to protect them against the might of Te Rauparaha. Even non-signers like the Ngati Kahungunu in the Hawke's Bay, did co-operate and compete to lease and sell land in the 1840s and 1850s. Pakeha brought trade with them and therefore wealth.

Maori still felt in control, and able to accept the ongoing partnership. Hone Heke wrote to the trader Gilbert Mair ticking him off for using trees from a tapu place and inviting Europeans indiscriminately to settle. Heke was in charge and wanted Gilbert Mair to know it.

Some tribes, including Te Arawa and Tuwharetoa, who were opposed to the Treaty were generally ignored. Tainui and Ngati Porou had reservations. Those chiefs like Te Wherowhero and Te Kani-a-Takirau who refused to sign did not prevent others in the tribe from doing so. This political strategy of hedging one's bets protected the tribe by not signing, while encouraging others to sign so that the tribe would not miss out on any advantages.

Key Points

- Two forms of authority were brought into co-existence in 1840.

- Kawanatanga and rangatiratanga were not going to co-exist easily nor equally. Pakeha and Maori had quite different ideas about the law. Pakeha thought it meant one law (English law) for all. Many Maori thought it meant English law for the Pakeha, but tikanga Maori for Maori.

- Maori were in theory to be equal British subjects. But this was not what many Pakeha settlers had in mind. When they outnumbered Maori and got control of Parliament they enacted laws which undermined this clause.

- One of the characteristics of the Treaty was the special, somewhat paternalistic, relationship between Monarch and Maori.

Further Reading

'The Maori and the signing of the Treaty of Waitangi' by Judith Binney in *Towards 1990: Seven leading historians examine significant aspects of New Zealand history*, edited by David Green

The Treaty of Waitangi by Claudia Orange

Making Peoples: A History of the New Zealanders from Polynesian settlement to the end of the Nineteenth Century by James Belich

Chapter 5

After the Treaty and up to 1975

> The single thread that most illuminates the historical fabric of Maori and Pakeha contact has been Maori determination to maintain Maori autonomy and the Government's desire to destroy it . . .
>
> [*Waitangi Tribunal The Taranaki Report* — *Kaupapa Tuatahi*, pp 5–15 (Wai 143) GP Publications, Wellington]

Immediately after the Treaty was signed Maori still outnumbered Pakeha. Though the two races co-operated and interacted successfully many Pakeha resented having Maori in charge.

The Treaty and Pakeha sovereignty

At first the British Colonial Office tried to interpret the Treaty as meaning that any land not actually occupied by Maori should become Crown land. There was a strong reaction against this within New Zealand. The outnumbered settlers realised Maori would not stand for this. New Zealand Chief Justice Martin pointed out that it would be a breach of the national faith pledged at Waitangi and a violation of established law in dealing with native lands. He felt that such an interpretation would endanger the humanitarian values reflected in the 1840

Treaty. The Colonial Office backed off and accepted that Maori title had to be interpreted in the widest sense.

The terms of the Treaty were well known within New Zealand. They were printed in full by an Auckland newspaper in 1843, with an alternative English translation of the Maori text. All the discussion on the Treaty and how to interpret it upset Maori. However, they were persuaded by officials of their special relationship with the Crown. This prompted direct appeals to Queen Victoria, for example against introduction of convicts, together with letters and gifts.

Early interaction

Those tribes nearest settlements interacted more with Pakeha than those in remote areas. Maori gardens provided Auckland and Wellington markets with produce and Maori worked on road-building. In turn they bought blankets, clothing, hardware, tobacco, soap, paper, arms, ammunition, boats and canvas from town shops. They had the reputation of being careful purchasers. Some adopted a European lifestyle, and settlements like Otaki and Rangiaowhia boasted extensive wheat fields, good barns, flour mills and numbers of cows and horses.

The new arrivals were mostly British, English-speaking, firmly believing that British law, government and culture was superior. They thought that the sooner the Maori assimilated themselves the better. Some did have a great deal of sympathy or admiration for Maori culture but most were arrogant, patronising or just overbearing.

Government

The Governor of the new colony was appointed by the British Government to administer justice and the new legal arrangements. Successive Governors often combined paternalism, such as supporting hospitals, with a policy of buying as much land as possible. But, like Sir George Grey, they also backed it up with threats or actual military force. Their aim was to extend Pakeha authority. But force was not always successful; in fact, there were some humiliating failures when Maori refused to be overawed by the new technology.

By 1856 the rapidly growing numbers of Pakeha began to outnumber the declining Maori population. The balance of power changed dramatically. The 1853 Constitution Act gave settlers the power to form a government and make their own laws. From then on laws were passed in the interests of the Pakeha majority. All adult males owning a small property could vote. Because communal ownership did not qualify as ownership for the purposes of voting, most Maori were excluded. Although four Maori seats were established in 1867, with language problems and small numbers, Maori never really had a chance to influence policy in Parliament in the 19th century.

Land and authority

Settlers coveted Maori lands. The rivalry between Maori and Pakeha became more open — it was about authority. Where land was owned by Pakeha, Pakeha law dominated; where Maori law and authority remained, as in the Waikato, it seemed to challenge the authority of the Government. By 1860 the European population had at 79,000 surpassed the declining Maori numbers. In the face of a growing reluctance by Maori to sell land and the supposed threat of a strong Maori King movement in the Waikato, Pakeha attitudes hardened.

When Governor Gore Browne called a Conference of Maori Chiefs together at Kohimarama in Auckland in 1860, he left out opposition chiefs from Taranaki and Waikato. His aim was to get support for a dubious land-purchasing policy in Taranaki. He tried to make Crown obligations under the Treaty conditional on Maori acceptance of Government authority. The meeting was reluctant to condemn the King movement. Many chiefs felt that there was room for both an independent Maori body and the Queen's sovereignty or mana. But the guarantees of the Treaty relating to forests and fisheries, not specified in the Maori text, were clarified. The Kohimarama covenant, the final resolution, was a solemn religious pledge, uniting Maori and Pakeha as one people. The Treaty had become too important to Maori to be ignored.

War

Meanwhile, disputes between the Government and the Ati Awa Taranaki chiefs over land sales had degenerated into war. Though Maori forces were greatly outnumbered, the Taranaki war ended in a stalemate. In Parliament and in newspapers, people like the Reverend Octavius Hadfield and Chief Justice Martin (now retired) criticised the Government's approach. But the challenge of an independent Maori authority in the Waikato sent shivers up the Pakeha spine.

The Governor, now Sir George Grey, manoeuvred the British Government into sending troops to attack the Waikato. He said they were planning an attack on Auckland. Even though total victory eluded the British and Colonial forces, the overall economic effect of the war on Maori communities was devastating. The rich lands of the Waikato were open to European exploitation.

After the wars

New laws were rushed through Parliament. They were based on the belief (grossly untrue) that most Maori — and the Waikato in particular — had plotted to exterminate the settlers. The New Zealand Settlements Act and Suppression of Rebellion Act (1863) sanctioned powers to arrest and detain immediately without habeas corpus, and trial by court martial. The excuse was that the Government needed unusual powers to deal with an emergency situation. Serious harm was done to Maori–Pakeha relations.

The Treaty was used as a justification for these measures. Frederick Whitaker, the Government leader in the Legislative Council (Upper House), justified the right to confiscate 'for public works'. He claimed it was part of the rights of sovereignty ceded by the Treaty. Maori as British subjects 'in rebellion' had no right of compensation. Military settlements in Waikato and Tauranga were established on confiscated land. This breach of the Treaty left a permanent legacy of bitterness. In Taranaki there followed a punitive campaign in which both innocent and fighting Maori had buildings destroyed and lost cultivations. The entire coastal strip of Taranaki was confiscated. Laws were passed designed to destroy any attempt to rival the authority of the Government and to superimpose British values. In the midst of this anti-Maori feeling there was always the idea that amalgamation was possible. But it had to be on Pakeha terms. One law for all it was said, but it was Pakeha law.

By 1874, Maori were only 14 percent of the total population. Legislation like the Native Lands Act 1865 and the Tohunga Suppression Act 1906 further disadvantaged Maori. Some legislation deliberately excluded Maori, at least to begin with. It was very difficult to get an old-age pension if you did not have a birth certificate. Land held in multiple ownership was not eligible for cheap loans for development. Maori found themselves penalised by local body rates. The Public Works Acts of 1864 and 1876 took land compulsorily for public development. The dog tax too was resented by Maori as infringing individual rights.

Attitudes to the Treaty

The Government did not want the Treaty resurrected. With the growth in the non-Maori population and the decline of the Maori population (only 45,470 in 1874) the Government could persuade itself that the Treaty had served its purpose, that New Zealand was a British colony by occupation. So official statements rarely praised and often disparaged the Treaty. The emphasis was on binding Maori to obey the law. But Maori never forgot the Treaty.

The courts

In the law courts too, the Treaty was under threat. In 1877, Maori owners who had given land to the Church of England for education, saw it was not being used for that purpose and wanted it back. The case went to court. This case, Wi Parata v. the Bishop of Wellington, had implications throughout New Zealand. The Maori owners' argument was based on their rights under the Treaty. Chief Justice James Prendergast ruled in favour of Pakeha interests. The Judge declared that the Treaty was a legal 'nullity' because it had not been incorporated in domestic law. His finding was that the Treaty meant nothing. Maori could not use the Treaty to claim customary land from the Crown.

Traditional fishing rights too were threatened by harbour development, drainage works and private ownership of land around rivers and lakes. Some allowance was made for Maori rights, but only for domestic consumption, not commercial use. Customary Maori fishing needs could be tolerated on the assumption that they were destined to fall into disuse because of the declining Maori population and assimilation.

Bledisloe's gift

In 1932 the gift of Busby's house and nearby land from Lord Bledisloe to the nation began the process of reviving Pakeha interest in the Treaty. Pakeha were always comfortable to think of the Treaty as a historical document. But its legal status was unchanged. In 1938 the Treaty could not be considered binding unless it were part of municipal law. It was, in Pakeha view, a quaint document, not part of the law and largely irrelevant.

Assimilation and integration

During the 1950s and 1960s there were several new laws affecting Maori adversely. The Maori Affairs Act 1953 disregarded traditional values, aiming at economic rationalisation and use of Maori land. It exacerbated tensions already caused by other legislation. Assimilation policies anticipated the end of a separate Maori identity. It was expected that intermarriage would create one people — some more brown than others.

In 1967, during the debates on the Maori Affairs Amendment Bill — a measure which was to alienate even more Maori land — the responsible Minister, the Hon. J. R. Hanan, saw it as:

> the most far-reaching and progressive reform of the Maori land laws this century . . . based upon the proposition that the Maori is the equal of the European . . . The Bill removes many of the barriers dividing our two people.

Another supporter of the Bill expressed the hope that 'it will mark the beginning of the end of what remains of apartheid in New Zealand'. Even integration policies looked very like assimilation.

The Treaty revived

But by the 1960s there was more interest in Waitangi and the Treaty. It had always been an important historical event to Pakeha, but with Maori insistence to make it more than an empty symbol, to give it real meaning, Pakeha too began to look at it again. The first step was official recognition of the date itself (see the following chapter for what happened next).

Maori Chieftainship: Tino Rangatiratanga and the Treaty

The other side of this history is the story of Maori attempts to hang on to some independence, to keep something of their own culture, language, and especially the land. Maori leaders tried in vain to influence those who made laws in Parliament, particularly the laws which aimed at separating them from their land and resources. Leaders who tried to do their own thing, like Te Whiti at Parihaka and Rua Kenana in the Urewera, found themselves up against the full force of Pakeha law. But most Maori accepted the new sovereignty, tried to use the system, and called upon the Treaty to protect themselves and their land against the Pakeha juggernaut. However, leaders who tried to co-operate found it difficult if not impossible to make themselves heard. Even as the Treaty was being signed, some Maori expressed concern.

One chief, as he asked what was going to be done about the traders who lied and cheated and stole, said: 'Yesterday I was cursed by a white man. Is this the way things are going to be?'

At first it was a matter of reminding settlers that Maori warriors could not be pushed around. So the tough, wily old warrior Te Rauparaha and his nephew Te Rangihaeata stopped Nelson settlers encroaching on Maori land in the Wairau plains in Marlborough. A posse of settlers went out to teach them a lesson — a fatal mistake for the 22 who were killed. In the North, Hone Heke objected to the economic rivalry of Auckland and the imposition of customs dues, both of which had reduced trade and the prosperity of the Bay of Islands. Cutting down the flagstaff at Russell was bad enough, but the outbreak of war was a difficult challenge for Governor FitzRoy. His replacement, Sir George Grey, was more successful, though he merely limited rather than crushed the potential challenge to the Pakeha Government.

The grievances

As settlers flooded in to take up land, chiefs became concerned at being overrun. Te Wharepouri, the Te Ati Awa chief in Wellington, complained that he had expected nine or 10 settlers when he sold his land. Within six months there were 13 ships and 1300 Pakeha. By the 1850s there was an occasional Maori appeal to the Queen about their grievances. This appeal to the Queen about Treaty rights became the pattern for the future.

In 1857, at a Rangiriri meeting, these grievances were spelt out. Lower-class whites were openly rude to chiefs, Maori women were being debauched, the liquor trade was destructive, and Maori bitterly resented the Pakeha habit of calling them 'Bloody Maoris'. Te Waharoa Wiremu Tamihana Tarapipipi, one of the paramount chiefs, had been kept waiting at the Native Office when Pakeha who had arrived after him were attended to first.

Restricting land sales

By 1858, the Pakeha population of 59,000 surpassed the Maori population of 56,000. The policy of restricting land sales — pupuri whenua — was widely discussed at intertribal meetings between 1853 and 1858. Chiefs tried to close off immigration by withholding land from sale. Te Rangitake (Wiremu Kingi) of Taranaki expressed Maori concerns very clearly as he dealt with an attempt by Governor Gore Browne to manoeuvre him into selling land:

> These lands will not be given by us into the Governor's and your hands lest we resemble the sea birds which perch upon a rock; when the tide flows the rock is covered by the sea, and the birds take flight for they have no resting place.

The King movement

Worries about losing land and power led to the election of Te Wherowhero of Waikato as the Maori King in 1858. He took the title of Potatau I. He was an aged warrior chief connected by his whakapapa to many important tribes. His own tribe was effectively blocking the advance of Pakeha into the central North Island, and he sent warriors to assist the Taranaki tribes in their struggle. He said:

> Let Maungatautari be our boundary. Do not encroach on this side — likewise I am not to set foot on that side.

Maori control over almost two-thirds of the North Island, and fears that further land would not be available for purchase, was seen as a challenge by the Pakeha Government. It seemed to be deliberate opposition to Queen Victoria. The moderate Maori view was that there was room for both.

War

War broke out first in Taranaki and then in the Waikato. When the fighting ended the Kingites withdrew south of the autaki, the new boundary of the confiscated lands. But the losses were indeed great. The most fertile lands of the Waikato were lost, either by confiscation or sale. Rich agricultural areas like Rangiaowhia were lost. Rangiaowhia, in spite of its status as a safe haven for old people and children during the war, had been sacked and burnt. Lost too, was the profitable trade with Auckland.

The Ngai Te Rangi Tribe had a stunning victory against impossible odds at Gate Pa, Tauranga, which slowed down the progress of the British Army. But they too had land confiscated. In the confused battles and civil wars which followed, often sparked off by the unfairness of confiscation, South Taranaki, devastated by British troops in a punitive expedition, became a wasteland. Leaders like Titokowaru, Te Kooti and Te Ua Haumene became embroiled in personal and local issues which limited their effectiveness.

When Te Waharoa Wiremu Tamihana Tarapipipi laid down his arms in 1865, he argued it was possible to have both Queen and King. In 1865 he petitioned the Queen, and in 1866 asked for a commission of enquiry into the confiscations. He asked the Queen to

> . . . give us back our land our chieftainship and our mana of which the colonists and the Governor are seeking to deprive us . . .

He also requested the Assembly to return all confiscated Waikato lands. They had to accept his petition because he was after all a British subject, but they gave him the runaround.

Different approaches

After 1870, Maori turned to a number of different approaches to regroup. All these approaches increasingly looked to the Treaty to find support. Warfare had failed. Even those hapu who had not signed the Treaty in 1840 turned to it as a basis for protection.

Turning to the courts

Some leaders, such those in the Hawke's Bay, tried to use the Pakeha system of law to obtain justice. They wanted to overturn deceitful purchases of land. This campaign, which emphasised the Treaty, became known as the Repudiation Movement. They had no success.

In 1879 a national Maori committee threatened legal action to test the validity of confiscations. The Government promptly appointed a commission of inquiry to prevent them. When Ngati Ruanui said that they had not signed the Treaty therefore their land had been illegally confiscated, the Government said that they had rights of sovereignty by discovery.

Turning to runanga

What does it mean?

Runanga = the ancient word for intertribal negotiations, used for meetings to decide matters of interest, usually involving local issues such as land ownership or the right to sell.

Runanga were held in an effort to get the Government to listen. These meetings all referred to the Treaty of Waitangi. They wanted to restrict further sales of land, possible only with a degree of self-government.

Ngati Whatua tried to hold another Kohimarama conference with the Government but it wasn't interested. A conference at Orakei in 1879 discussed the Treaty. Maori were disillusioned with the Government attitude. They were particularly concerned about the loss of fishing rights. Later conferences looked back to the 1835 Declaration of Independence, which they saw as having recognised some degree of self-government.

By the 1880s the King Movement of the Waikato was coming to terms with the Pakeha Government. Te Wherowhero Tawhiao, the second Maori King, challenged the Government's interpretation of the Treaty of Waitangi. It was not correct, he stated, that all power had been given to the Pakeha. Maori, like Pakeha, had the right to govern themselves. In 1894, the Kauhanganui (the King's Great Council), claiming to speak for all Maori, declared that confiscated land belonged by right to Maori, and that relationships between Maori and Pakeha should be ordered under the Treaty on the basis of equality. It was keen to emphasise that it was not in conflict with the covenant of the Queen in the Treaty.

In the North, Te Tii Marae was becoming the place for Nga Puhi to gather. A new marae building — 'The Treaty of Waitangi' — was opened in 1881. The full text of the Treaty was inscribed at the base of a monument, to remind the Government of its obligations. A runanga discussed the return of confiscated lands, the rights to the foreshore, the unpopular dog tax, and the Government's handling of Parihaka. There were 3000 Maori present. The hospitality was lavish, the publicity wide, but the response from the government was disappointing.

In 1892, a Kotahitanga Parliament was formally set up at

Waitangi, also claiming to speak for all Maori. The Kotahitanga Parliament did not reject British culture. It wanted to improve the laws, not to block settlement. Those present wanted to decide for themselves what to borrow and at what speed. Government responded by setting up the Maori Councils Act of 1900, which diverted support away from the Kotahitanga.

Turning to independent living

At Parihaka in South Taranaki, Te Whiti o Rongomai and Tonu Kakahi led passive resistance to the confiscation of land, distressed that the Government had not kept its promise to set aside reserves of land for Maori. Their settlement was a model of co-operative living based on non-violence and religious precepts. This village of peace provided a haven for all the morehu (ordinary people, the underprivileged) of war-weary tribes, who came to learn the teachings of the prophets.

All roads led to Parihaka. The small community swelled to over 2000 people. Opening up the Waimate Plain to Pakeha farmers threatened Parihaka's survival. Government surveyors found their pegs pulled out and the land ploughed. Parihaka became the focus of resistance to the Pakeha. At the same time, Pakeha attitudes hardened. The settlers were indignant and outraged. False rumours grew that the settlement of Parihaka was fortified.

In 1881, 1600 armed constables led by John Bryce, Minister of Native Affairs, marched on Parihaka. The prophets were imprisoned and the village dismantled. This pahua (plunder) of their village effectively destroyed the strength of Parihaka. The message was clear. Separate development was a threat to Pakeha authorities.

A similar message was received in 1916 by Rua Kenana Hepetika, a Tuhoe leader who developed a community at Maungapohatu, a remote spot in the Urewera. It was a model community, peaceful and progressive, with the aim of modernising trade and agriculture. But it rejected Pakeha laws and taxes. A trumped-up charge of flouting the liquor laws sent constables out to arrest Rua. A scuffle followed in which two were killed including one of Rua's sons, and Rua himself was imprisoned after a questionable trial. The weakened community never recovered its vibrancy.

Turning to the Queen or King of England

Maori leaders appealed directly to the Queen in England and later to her successors. Petitioners, including King Tawhaio and Nga Puhi chiefs, asked for investigations into the confiscation of land and for some self-government. They based their appeals on their rights under the Treaty. They were referred back to the New Zealand Parliament. But the New Zealand Government remained deaf.

Turning to Parliament

In 1867 four seats in Parliament were allocated to Maori. In 1868, Mete Kingi Paetahi spoke on Maori grievances in Maori. With only four seats out of 70 and debates in English, parliamentary representation was not of much use to Maori until the 1890s. Anyway, some tribes and hapu felt unrepresented. In the 1880s more than a thousand Maori petitions, many of them featuring the Treaty, were presented to the General Assembly. The four Maori MPs also appealed ineffectually to the Aborigines Protection Society in 1883. In 1919, three Maori MPs forwarded a copy of the Treaty to the British Government. It was received with some puzzlement but filed.

New leaders

Towards the end of the 19th century a new group of Western-educated leaders emerged to bridge the gap between Pakeha and Maori. These men like James Carroll, Apirana Ngata, Maui Pomare and Te Rangi Hiroa (Peter Buck), were able to succeed in both a Maori world and a Pakeha world. Through their careers in medicine, politics and anthropology, they were able to improve relationships between Maori and Pakeha. Apirana Ngata, for example, was able to persuade the Government to spend some money on improving Maori farming. But in the Supreme Court, Maori plaintiffs were continuing to lose cases with claims based on the Treaty. Clearly what was needed was formal recognition of the Treaty.

Ratana

In the 1920s a new Maori leader emerged. This was Tahupotiki Wiremu Ratana, a faith healer whose religious and political vision appealed to ordinary people. With strong leadership he succeeded in building an enduring church from his Wanganui base. In the 1930s he made an Alliance with the Labour Party. He was an important advocate for the Treaty. He wanted the Treaty incorporated in law, and had even taken a petition to England in 1924, only to be referred back to New Zealand. In 1932 the first Ratana MP, Eruera Tirikatene, presented a petition containing over 30,000 signatures asking that the Treaty be made part of the law.

In 1934, Nga Puhi hosted a grand ceremony to celebrate the Treaty and to mark 100 years since Britain had acknowledged Maori sovereignty. After the Second World War, many Maori moved to the cities and towns in search of new opportunities and employment. But in spite of government policies of assimilation, many did not want to become brown-skinned Pakeha. Old grievances were not forgotten and the loss of the land in particular was felt keenly. Economic disparities served to remind people of their loss. Meanwhile, Ratana voices in the Labour caucus had put the Treaty firmly on the political agenda.

As the protest movement gathered strength in the 1960s and 1970s, Maori MPs were able to focus public debate on the Treaty. Both the leading political parties, National and Labour, came to realise that a new look at the Treaty was needed. It had to become more than a symbol; it had to have real meaning if any progress was to be made.

> In the words of Judge (now Justice) E. T. Durie:
> It needs to be understood that if the Treaty was assigned to the garbage can by lawyers and politicians, it was never accorded that treatment in Maoridom. It has dominated Maori political debate from the 1840s to the present day. Throughout history large gatherings of Maori people have been called to discuss that one topic. It has been the subject of countless petitions to Parliament and the Courts. Modern Maori debate on the Treaty is certainly nothing new.
> [Te Oru Rangahau Maori Research and Development Conference, 7–9 July 1998, Massey University]

Key Points

- The Treaty and its guarantees have always been important to Maori.
- Until the late 20th century, many Pakeha considered the Treaty to be a quaint, irrelevant historical document.
- The courts and Parliament did not accept the Treaty as part of the law.
- Many Maori have always wanted to retain a separate identity, not to be swallowed up by Pakeha culture.

Further Reading

Nga Iwi o Te Motu: 1000 Years of Maori History by Michael King

An Unsettled History: Treaty Claims in New Zealand Today by Alan Ward

Chapter 6

The Crucial Issue of Land

Why has land always been such an issue?

Whatu ngarongaro te tangata
Toitu te whenua

(People perish but the land is permanent)

Maori land

In the Maori world every natural feature of the land had a name describing some feature of the long centuries of occupation. Every part of New Zealand was owned. Every tribe, every hapu, had its own sacred places where perhaps the talisman of the tribe was hidden. At birth the child's umbilical cord was buried with rituals illustrating the connection with the land. With a child of rank, a tree was often planted, later to serve as a marker in disputes over land ownership.

All land was held in common by the hapu. Individuals did not own land though they had the right to occupy, use or cultivate certain areas, with the agreement of the hapu. To maintain ownership to the land it had to be occupied, used and defended. The tribal chief could alienate land but only after a consensus decision by the tribe.

> Under New Zealand law there are three types of Maori land:
>
> **Customary:** land originally owned before title was determined by the Native Land Court. This now only covers a few rocky barren islands. The Maori attitude is that the Crown should have to prove its title to all Crown land, and if it cannot, title should revert to the Maori owners.
>
> **Reserved:** reserves set aside on behalf of the original Maori owners during the 19th century, to be administered by the Crown in trust for the Maori owners.
>
> **Maori freehold land:** land that comes under the Maori Land Court. It is about 5 percent of New Zealand, although it is difficult to distinguish exactly what is Maori and what is general land (Pakeha-owned), as some Maori own both.

Land sales

During the 19th century most of the land held by Maori was sold to the Pakeha. Some was bought by the Crown and some was confiscated after the wars. Still more was sold through the Native Land Court. This court, set up by Parliament with no Maori representation (before 1867) and without consultation, revolutionised traditional land tenure, converting communal holdings into individual tenure. All these processes were often unjust and unfair. They have left Maori with a strong sense of grievance and resulted in many claims to the Waitangi Tribunal.

> Amount of land in Maori title, 1840:
> 26,892,000 ha/66,400,000 acres

Even before the Treaty of Waitangi, Maori were willing and even eager to sell land. Getting onto the land-selling bandwagon was

> **Maori Land Court**
> The Maori Land Court, originally called the Native Land Court, holds the records of Maori land ownership since 1862. In the late 20th century it became a Maori institution and a force for retention of land. It administers Te Ture Whenua Maori Act 1993/the Maori Land Act 1993, settles succession matters, deals with transfers, and works out differences between owners.

a way of making sure your hapu did not miss out; a way of asserting a claim to the land. So land sales were a means of continuing the usual interhapu or intertribal competition.

Many of these early sellers probably did not understand the European view of the transaction. How could you take seriously people who left goods and a pile of blankets on the shore and then disappeared? Maori knew that land had to be occupied and defended militarily. Anyway, dealings with land were about relationships with others. For Muriwhenua, for example, the transactions or contracts with Europeans in the pre-Treaty period were about encouraging European settlement. Where one race thought they were making a transaction about the permanent transfer of land, the other race was making a contract to include newcomers into their social unit and defining their mutual relationship. They were both talking past each other.

After the Treaty of Waitangi

After the Treaty many of these early purchases were investigated. Various Europeans including the New Zealand Company (organised by E. G. Wakefield, based on the idea of buying land cheaply from Maori and selling it dear to new immigrants) claimed to have bought vast tracts of land. In some cases land stayed with the Maori, but where the sale was considered valid the Government imposed a restriction of 'no more than 2560 acres' to a claimant. The surplus was taken by the Crown, not returned to Maori. Present-day claims to the Waitangi Tribunal have challenged both the findings of the investigators and the actions of the Crown in keeping the surplus. The Tribunal has found that for Muriwhenua, where the best land was bought even before the Treaty was signed, government investigations of the so-called purchases were quite inadequate.

> ### Hobson's orders
> The British Government had instructed Hobson that tribes were to keep enough land to support them in the future. Hobson was told that Maori must not be allowed to enter into any deals or contracts in which they might be the 'ignorant and unintentional authors of injuries to themselves'.

Sales to the Crown

The Treaty's second clause gave the Crown the exclusive right — or at least the first option, the meaning was never quite clear — to purchase land. Although this clause was designed to protect Maori from unscrupulous dealers it was also used to fund emigration, by buying land cheap and selling it at a higher cost. The profits were used to bring out more settlers. When it suited them, Governors suspended the clause.

Governors like Sir George Grey tried to buy as much land as possible. Grey's land-purchasing agents were entitled 'Commissioners for the extinguishment of native title by fair purchase'. They bought almost all the South Island and huge blocks of land in Auckland, Hawke's Bay and the Manawatu. Grey and his land buyer Donald McLean purchased 32.6 million acres — nearly half the whole country. The average price paid was less than a halfpenny an acre. However, these Government purchases were not always fair and above board.

There were shady deals. Some have led to claims under the Tribunal.

> 1852: 13,770,000 ha/34,000,000 acres in Maori hands

Though land buying had been successful in the South Island and in Northern areas, Maori still controlled the best farmland in the North Island. Maori farming had been very successful in the 1840s and early 1850s. They had supplied the Australian market with wheat, and Maori produce was sold in Auckland and other early settlements. But a dramatic fall in agricultural prices and competition from Pakeha farmers after 1856 saw the market collapse. With Pakeha farmers turning to pastoral farming there was an increased demand for Maori land. But this coincided with an anti-land-selling movement in the Waikato and Taranaki as Maori chiefs realised how Pakeha ownership was threatening their mana. The anti-selling movement was a mixed success for Maori; Waikato was more successful than Taranaki. But the threat of an independent, strong, separate Maori authority across the centre of the North Island was too much for the Government, and confrontation led to war. The real issue was about who would control the new society. Where Maori owned the land, Maori authority dominated. For Pakeha, victory gave them the important prize of the fertile North Island lands.

> 1860: 8,667,000 ha/21,400,000 acres in Maori hands

Confiscation

The New Zealand Settlements Act and Suppression of Rebellion Act 1863 gave the Government wide-ranging powers to confiscate tribal lands and put settlers on them. Tribes classified as rebels had their land taken. However, both friendly Maori, fighting with the Government, and rebels lost their lands. Over three million acres were taken in the

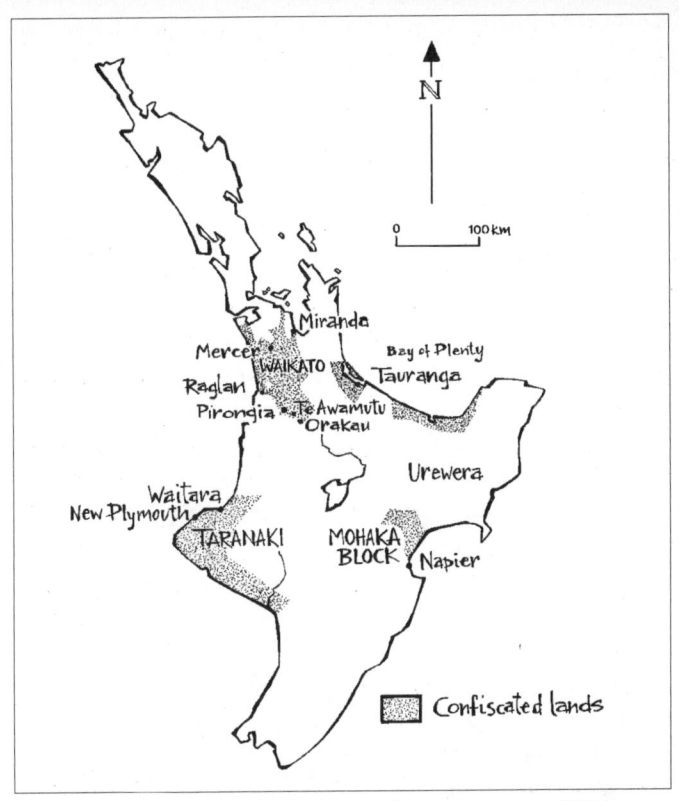

Areas of Maori land confiscated in the 1860s, under the 1863 New Zealand Settlements Act and Suppression of Rebellion Act

Waikato, Bay of Plenty and Taranaki. About half was given back, but not always to the right people, and it was often the inferior, less important land that was returned. Confiscation fell unevenly. The Waikato lost almost everything, while Ngati Maniapoto went untouched. Confiscation left a legacy of bitterness.

> The Crown now accepts that this confiscation of land was an injustice and in breach of the Principles of the Treaty.

THE CRUCIAL ISSUE OF LAND 71

The Native Land Court

The Native Lands Act 1865, which ended the Government's right of pre-emption, established the Native Land Court. Its job was to decide who owned the land, to transfer the communal title into individual ownership, and make it easier for settlers to buy the land. The Court followed British legal conventions, leaving little room for Maori forms of justice, evidence and debate. It turned Maori land ownership on its head. Politicians and judges thought that it was in the best interests of the Maori to amalgamate. They believed in private property and thought Maori would get the same benefits from individual title that Europeans did.

A parcel of land was identified as belonging to a hapu. The Court then apportioned shares. But only up to 10 names could go on the title and only the heirs of those 10 would inherit. This left out many members of the hapu, and their rights were not always taken into account by the 10 named on their behalf in the hapu, who became the owners. Many were left landless and disinherited.

The Court process was long and costly. Reluctant chiefs found themselves in debt and obliged to sell. Unscrupulous techniques were used to separate Maori from their land. The Court did much to destroy Maori society. Obliged to live away from home for months, getting into debt, vulnerable to the land-purchasing rings exploiting disputes between rival claimants, squandering money advanced by purchase agents, there were serious human consequences for Maori applicants. No wonder that it was tribal areas which had little to do with Pakeha that were thriving, while depopulation was marked in areas where the Land Court operated.

> The Crown now acknowledges that this Court had a widespread and enduring impact on Maori society and that it breached its responsibilities under the Treaty.

Grievances before the Waitangi Tribunal

Many Maori grievances that come before the Tribunal relate to this period. The claims are often very vague and difficult to assess. The loss of the land has become a symbol of Maori protest. Though loss of the economic resource appears to be the issue, underlying this is a more general distress about losing touch with each other, no longer being fluent in Maori, or perhaps no longer having a marae. Even those who have been successful in the city share this sense of loss, even if it was partly the fault of individual ancestors in the hapu who sold off hapu lands and did not distribute the profits.

> 1891: 4,487,192 ha/11,079,486 acres in Maori hands

A later law divided a deceased owner's interest among all the descendants. In Maori tradition, the right to the land lapsed if a descendant 'let his fire die out'. Ignoring this tradition led to fragmentation of land ownership. It is now not uncommon for blocks of land to be owned by thousands of shareholders scattered throughout the country.

> By 1896 only 4,455,000 ha/11 million acres were left out of 26.9 million ha/66.4 million acres.

During the second half of the 19th century heavy demand for pastoral land led to the further transfer of three million acres of land to Pakeha ownership. Government and Maori had very different views on how much land should be kept and how to handle land still in Maori ownership. Those farming Maori-owned land got very little help. There was always the threat that one of the co-owners would want to sell. At a time when Pakeha farmers were getting cheap loans for purchase and development, titles surveyed and road access provided (Lands for Settlements Act 1892, Advances to Settlers Act 1894), Maori farmers were not eligible and were left to struggle alone.

1911: 2,890,568 ha/7,137,205 acres in Maori hands

Ninety years after the Treaty, in the late 1920s, at last some help was given to Maori land schemes. Sir Apirana Ngata, Native Minister from 1928–1934, attempted to use land development to create a sound economic base for tribes. Other Maori leaders like Princess Te Puea were able to show that collective strategy was successful. Setting up incorporations and trusts helped. Incorporations, where the tribe formed a committee which acted as a board of directors, given legal recognition in 1909, have since been important for land development. Trusts gave management to trustees as a way to handle multiple ownership.

1920: 1,939,013 ha/4,787,686 acres in Maori hands

But Maori farmers continued to be bedevilled with fragmentation of titles, limited access to development funding, poor representation on agriculture producer boards, and even poorer access to farming information. Their lands of marginal quality were often too small to be a productive unit.

1939: 1,631,706 ha/4,028,903 acres in Maori hands

After World War II many Maori migrated to the city in search of employment. Population growth and shortage of land stimulated the migration but Moari did not lose interest in the land. Land ownership gave social status and spiritual identification. Turangawaewae remained an important concept.

What does it mean?

Turangawaewae = the place where I stand. Gives one the right to belong and participate on home marae. It indicates close connections between land, tribal and

personal identity, and mana. It symbolises identity as a
Maori, and the self-esteem and pride in being one.

Pakeha values

New Zealand Pakeha values, on the other hand, place great importance on efficient agricultural production. Land should be easily available, put to good use and made to work. Multiple ownership and sentiment about land have no place in this view — they are an obstruction. Many government investigations perpetuated the view that development needs override other considerations, and that Maori land was hindered by fragmentation and by Maori cultural attitudes. The Prichard-Waetford Report of 1965, for example, said:

> Fragmentalism is a euphemism for having too many owners in a block of land. The only way to deal with the problem is to reduce the number of owners.

So the Maori Affairs Amendment Act 1967 made provision for Maori land to be converted to general land if held by not more than four joint owners. Also, a Maori Trustee could sell Maori lease lands even if not all the owners agreed. The legislation was repealed in 1974 but not before 96,000 hectares had been compulsorily converted to general land.

Reserved land

The Crown's handling of reserved lands was seen as a most glaring injustice. Some reserves were sold, others used for Crown purposes such as universities, while others were leased in perpetuity. These totalled 27,600 ha in 1977. Towns such as Rotorua and Te Kuiti were built on Maori land. By 1996, lands leased in perpetuity totalled 26,000 hectares with an estimated value of $200 million. The 2236 leases included farmlands, commercial sites and urban residential properties. The effect of Crown administration has been to deny Maori access to their lands. They were seldom consulted about the terms of the lease or the distribution of the benefits. The interests of the lessees have been favoured over the interests of the owners.

In 1991 a review team heard submissions from owners and lessees, and proposed a long-term plan to return ownership to Maori and to buy back improvements. They wanted to bring rents up to market rates without compensation, and with more frequent reviews. Neither owners nor lessees were happy. Maori were appalled by the delay and lack of compensation; lessees were furious about increased rents and demanded compensation. The Maori Reserved Land Amendment Act 1996 did give compensation to the lessees for the loss of their perpetual rights of renewal. However, Maori owners were told to claim compensation through the Waitangi Tribunal.

In the 1970s land issues made all New Zealanders aware of the need for action. The publicity given to the 1975 Land March and the occupation of Bastion Point in 1977 could not be overlooked.

> 1975: Waitangi Tribunal formed — around 3 million acres (1,323,564 ha) remained as tribal estates

Land march

In 1975, Matakite o Aotearoa led a Land March of 30,000 from the northern tip of the North Island to Parliament in Wellington to present to the Prime Minister a Memorial of Rights petitioning government to stop the unjust alienation of land. The slogan was 'Not one more acre of land'. It demonstrated the extent of Maori dissatisfaction and their desire to take action. In front marched Whina Cooper (first president of the Maori Women's Welfare League).

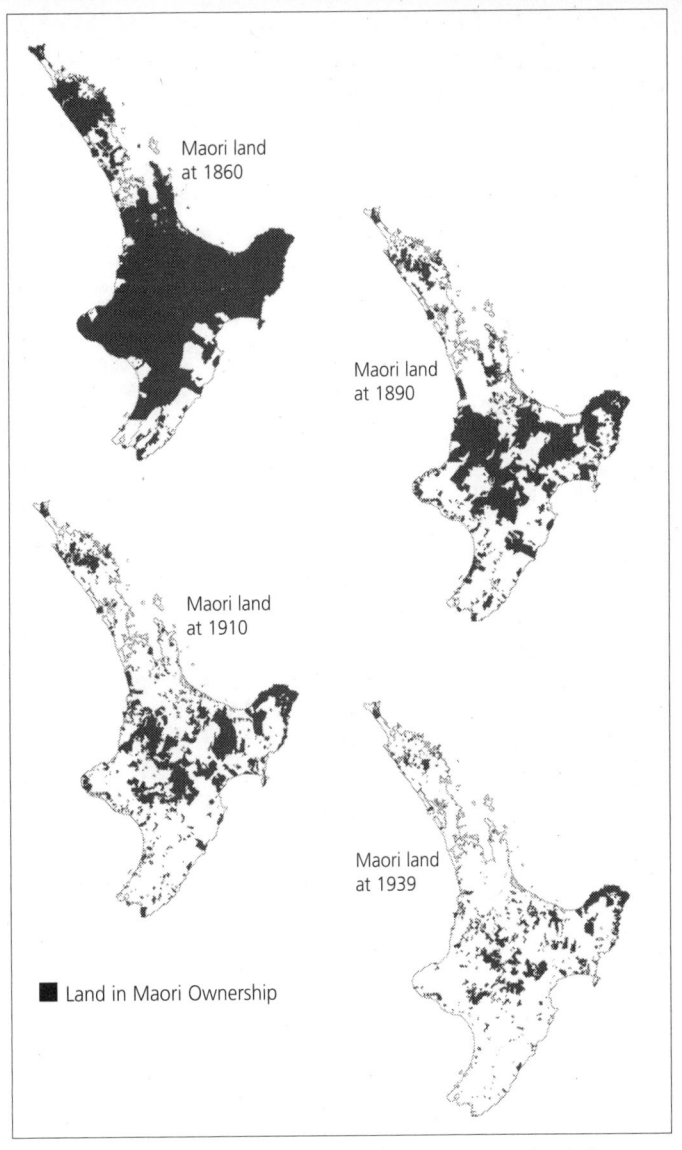

The extent of alienation of Maori land in the North Island after the signing of the Treaty of Waitangi

THE CRUCIAL ISSUE OF LAND 77

Bastion Point occupation

In 1977 a group from Ngati Whatua occupied Bastion Point. There was a Government plan to subdivide 24 hectares of Crown land (with to-die-for harbour views) for upmarket residential use. But behind this decision was a long history of dispossession and oppression. The Orakei Maori Action Committee, with support from some other tribal members, trade union movements, the Matakite movement, Whina Cooper and the Citizens Association for Racial Equality, established a camp at Bastion Point.

> #### History of Bastion Point land
> The Orakei Native Reserve Act 1882 had disregarded earlier promises to protect land for the tribe and allowed for long-term leasing. By 1898 the inalienable reserve had been reduced from 280 hectares to 15.6 hectares. In 1951 residents were evicted from their papakainga (home village) and put into state houses in Kitemoana Street. With total disregard for Maori opinion, the Government was determined to drive Ngati Whatua out of prime real estate in one of Auckland's most prestigious suburbs.

But occupation leader Joe Hawke and the new generation were not prepared to accept the Government's proposal for subdivision. During the occupation, Maori opinion was divided as to the best methods of action. The Government sought to make agreement with the more moderate elders by the return of 13 hectares and some $200,000 in cash. Protestors felt that the moderates were selling out. Bastion Point was being used as a focus for other tribal dissatisfactions. After an occupation of 506 days, protestors swelled in number from 150 to many more. A court ruling led to an eviction, with over 200 protesters arrested by 600 policemen and army personnel. Eventually in

1991 the Crown accepted the more realistic recommendations of the Waitangi Tribunal. Joe Hawke joined the ranks of Ngati Whatua establishment and later became an MP for Labour.

So the 20th century too had witnessed large-scale loss of land, by such means as the Maori Land Boards, the Board of Maori Affairs and other government agencies as well as the Land Court. Approximately 3.5 million acres were sold between 1910 and 1930. A great deal more was leased during this period. Grievances also arose from Crown actions concerning Maori Land Development and Consolidation schemes.

There were also grievances concerning the gifting of land for specific purposes like schools. In many cases the Crown has not returned the land to the rightful owners once the purpose has been fulfilled, but has used it for other purposes or even sold it. Under Public Works Acts, particularly in the 19th century, Maori owners were frequently disadvantaged. Land was taken for roads without compensation. Many hapu lost wahi tapu (sacred places) such as urupa (burial grounds) or were left landless. Sometimes taonga were destroyed or acquired in a dubious manner. All these grievances have featured in claims before the Waitangi Tribunal.

Current land policy

Today the emphasis is on keeping the land in Maori ownership. The 1993 Te Ture Whenua Maori Act, passed after extensive consultation, is based on the Treaty of Waitangi and recognises that Maori land is a taonga tuku iho, an asset inherited from earlier generations. The purpose of the Act is to retain the land so that it is passed on to future generations. It has made Maori land more difficult to alienate. At the same time, it provides greater opportunity for owners to make maximum commercial use of their land.

Key Points

- ❖ Loss of the land has been the principal focus of Maori grievances.

- ❖ The Crown has not kept the promises about land made in the Treaty and in many cases it needs to make amends.

- ❖ Dubious land sales, failure to set aside the promised reserved land, confiscation of land, overturning of the traditional tenure system and mismanagement of existing reserves have severely disadvantaged Maori.

- ❖ Much of New Zealand's current wealth has been based on the exploitation of resources obtained unjustly.

Further Reading

The Waitangi Tribunal Reports such as the Muriwhenua Land Report, 1999 or Te Whanganui a Tara me ona Takiwa: Report on the Wellington District, 2003

'Te Kooti tango whenua': The Native Land Court 1864–1909 by David V. Williams

Maori Land by George Asher and David Naulls

Chapter 7

The Waitangi Tribunal 1975

During the 1980s there was a big change in the Government's approach to Maori policy, reflecting a change of attitude in the community. What brought about this new focus?

Disparities

First there were economic disparities between Pakeha and Maori. On almost all socio-economic indices there were big differences between Maori and non-Maori. In areas such as participation in secondary schooling, tertiary education, standards of health, and income levels, there had been improvements, but Maori were still trailing behind non-Maori. With the restructuring of the 1980s, Maori unemployment (even in 1996) at 16 percent ended up more than twice as high as the non-Maori rate. And despite a range of initiatives from the state and from Maori themselves, Maori were still disproportionately represented in the poorer paid and insecure jobs.

Some individuals, however, were and still are doing very well. Each whanau had a few members who are well qualified and prosperous. However, the vast majority were still at the bottom of the economic heap. But there was nothing new in this disparity. What else was happening?

Maori became more determined. They had become more familiar with political and legal processes. They became more assertive in their desire to secure redress for past and current breaches of the Treaty, to overcome Maori social and economic disadvantage. Well-established national groups often took the lead. There was more general interest in the issues. Local academics were doing more research. Other countries too, like Canada, showed the way. There, indigenous peoples had achieved some recognition of customary rights.

Waitangi Day

But perhaps the crucial factor was Waitangi Day itself. There was very real, popular pressure for Waitangi Day to be a ritual of greater significance. Maori saw this as the first step in getting the Treaty recognised legally. Even the most irritatingly strident protests were getting the point across. Pakeha had concentrated for years on Waitangi Day as a day of historical importance; now the pressure was on to make it mean something to contemporary New Zealanders.

This revival of interest meant that a number of groups wanted to take another look at the Treaty itself, to celebrate the day. Government policy and government agencies were moving towards greater responsiveness to Maori aspirations. In this context, the Waitangi Tribunal was set up.

> *Waitangi Day*
> **1932** *Lord Bledisloe, the incumbent Governor-General, presented Busby's house and 1000 acres at Waitangi to the nation as a national memorial. This gift helped to revive Pakeha interest in the Treaty.*
> **1946–7** *A new flagpole was erected and annual naval ceremonies began.*
> **1948** *A government grant helped subsidise entry fees to the Treaty House.*
> **1953** *Queen Elizabeth II made a brief visit, beginning the tradition of royal visits and annual attendance on 6 February by the Governor-General.*
> **1960** *6 February was to be known as Waitangi Day, a 'national day of thanksgiving in commemoration of the signing'. Any region could substitute it for an existing holiday.*
> **1973** *The Labour Government made Waitangi Day a public holiday on the day of the week it fell. It was to be called New Zealand Day.*
> **1976** *The name was changed back to Waitangi Day.*

The Waitangi Tribunal 1975–1985

The Treaty of Waitangi Act 1975, sponsored by the Minister of Maori Affairs, Matiu Rata, gave the Tribunal authority to hear claims by Maori who believed they were prejudicially affected by legislation, policies or practices of the Crown that were inconsistent with the principles of the Treaty of Waitangi. If the Tribunal found a claim to be substantiated it could recommend action that could be taken by the Crown to provide a redress or remedy.

The Tribunal was given the authority to determine the meaning and effect of the Treaty, but the Act excluded anything done (or not done) before 1975. The Tribunal had the status of a permanent Commission of Inquiry. This meant it could order witnesses to come before it, order documents or other material to be produced, and actively search out material and facts. The Tribunal has to send copies of its findings and recommendations to Ministers of the Crown and to the claimant. Apart from orders for the resumption of land, the Tribunal's recommendations are not binding on the Crown. But the Government always takes them very seriously.

> ### What is the Crown?
> The Crown is the executive branch of government. The other two branches are Parliament (the legislature) and the courts (judiciary). The Crown therefore includes the Monarch, the Governor-General, the Prime Minister and Ministers of the Cabinet, and the government departments of administration. Because they are responsible to the voters it can be said that the Crown symbolises the people of New Zealand.

Some key features of the Treaty of Waitangi Act 1975 (and later amendments)

- Claimants must be Maori or of Maori descent.
- Claims are made by individuals who may claim on behalf of a group.
- Only claims against the Crown can be heard.
- The claim must show how the claimant has been prejudicially affected by the Crown's actions or omissions.
- If the claim is too trivial, or there are better ways of solving the grievance, the Tribunal can refuse to inquire into it.

- It can hold hearings on a marae, and follows marae kawa (local custom) when it does so.
- Claimants can seek direct negotiations with the Crown once the claim is lodged. For direct negotiations the Crown prefers to deal with iwi, and insists that the claimant has an appropriate mandate.

What does it mean?

The term Maori is defined in the Treaty of Waitangi Act 1975 and means 'a person of the Maori race of New Zealand; and includes any descendant of such person.' This means that as long as a person can trace descent from a Maori ancestor, such a person may identify as Maori.

Principles established by the Crown for settling historical claims

- The Crown will explicitly acknowledge historical injustices, that is, grievances arising from Crown actions or omissions before 21 September 1992.
- Treaty settlements should not create further injustices.
- The Crown has a duty to act in the best interests of all New Zealanders.
- As settlements are to be durable, they must be fair, sustainable and remove the sense of grievance.
- The Crown must deal fairly and equitably with all claimant groups.
- Settlements do not affect Maori entitlements as New Zealand citizens, nor do they affect their ongoing rights arising out of the Treaty.

- Settlements will take into account fiscal and economic constraints and the ability of the Crown to pay compensation.

Maori critics pointed out that only two of these principles worry about fairness to claimants, while all the others emphasise reassurance for non-claimants. They were also concerned that Maori interests in natural resources were to be confined to use and value. Most tribes saw this refusal to contemplate Maori ownership of natural resources, even though acknowledging use and value interests, as contrary to the Treaty of Waitangi. The courts had recognised Maori interests in natural resources and have never explicitly ruled out Maori ownership. The conservation estate was also excluded from settlement arrangements under the assumption that it was owned by the Crown.

What does it mean?

Natural resources = water, geothermal energy, river and lake beds, foreshore and seabeds, sand and shingle and minerals such as gold, coal, gas and petroleum.

How the Tribunal proceeds

The Tribunal adopted an inquiry approach rather than an adversarial approach. It tries to avoid polarised positions. Claims are heard in Maori and in English and are weighed against the Maori and English versions of the Treaty signed in 1840. Claims by Maori are usually heard on the claimants' marae using local Maori protocol. Pakeha and Crown submissions are held in public buildings in nearby towns, using Pakeha procedures and protocols.

As the process has developed, the Crown has established more specific requirements before settlements are completed. It prefers to negotiate with iwi rather than hapu because of time and expense. It insists on a secure mandate on the part of a claimant group before negotiations can start. Equally, overlapping interests of different claimant groups have to be settled first. The Crown doesn't dictate how the assets are to be used but the iwi must have a governance structure which is representative, transparent and accountable. The settlements are final, not to be reopened by the courts, the tribunal or any other body.

Membership of the Tribunal

The Tribunal began with three members: the Chief Judge of the Maori Land Court as Chairman, one Maori on the recommendation of the Minister of Maori Affairs, and one other person on the recommendation of the Minister of Justice. The Tribunal has grown to a membership of 16, plus the Chief Judge of the Maori Land Court, or a High Court judge who is the Chairperson. Members, with a range of skills, are appointed for a three-year term by the Governor-General on the recommendation of the Minister of Maori Affairs and the advice of the Minister of Justice.

> ### Types of Claims
>
> **Historical (before 21 September 1992):** concerning the actions of the Crown in the past. These are mostly about land.
>
> **Contemporary (after 21 September 1992):** deals with present social and cultural issues and processes used by the Government. Examples are Maori language, resource management, education and immigration. These claims can also go to the courts or the relevant government agency.
>
> **Conceptual:** deals with Maori interests in the use and development of rivers, lakes, foreshores, minerals, geothermal resources, or outputs of these resources.

The Tribunal got off to a slow start with only 36 enquiries from 1975–1986. But in 1985 an important change was made, extending its jurisdiction from 1975 back to 1840. In 1987 alone there were 88 enquiries. By August 1991, 224 claims were registered. In March 1993 there were 300. By 1997 there were 633 claims. In 2004 the Tribunal estimates it is about halfway through the claims before it.

> ### Claim research
> *Before a claim is considered much research has to be done. The Tribunal has taken up a new approach of regional research, making broad historical surveys in each district. It is known as the* rangahaua whanau *and allows equal weighting to all historical claims, reduces duplication and gives a national overview. Researchers in the 15 districts use set criteria for evaluating the seriousness of Treaty breaches by the Crown. These are: acts of commission, acts of omission, demography, quantity, and value of the resource lost.*

Future claims over Crown land

When in the late 1980s, government policies favoured selling state assets to private individuals, Maori feared that the Government would then not be in a position to honour Treaty claims. They wanted land, rather than monetary compensation. So the Maori Council took legal action. The result was a landmark Court of Appeal case in 1987. The Court of Appeal ordered the Government to make provision to safeguard Maori interests in Crown land for future Treaty settlements. The Treaty of Waitangi (State Enterprises) Act, introduced in 1988, provided that land sold by the Crown to a State-Owned Enterprise would carry a memorial warning the purchaser that reversion to the Crown might be necessary to meet a Waitangi Tribunal order.

Changes in the Waitangi Tribunal since its establishment

- ❖ *1975* Claims can be made dating back to 6 February 1840; a Court of Appeal decision in favour of State-Owned Enterprise and Crown forest land being available for settling grievances also allowed the Tribunal to commission research and to receive reports on research as evidence; membership was expanded to six, four of whom were to be Maori — they could sit in divisions and consider separate claims simultaneously; deputy members could be appointed; an amendment also corrected errors in the Maori text of the Treaty which had appeared in the 1975 Act.

- ❖ *1988* The Tribunal may order repurchase of land transferred to State-Owned Enterprises if it is required to settle land claims; legal aid is available for claimants; membership of the Tribunal increased to 17 including the Chief Judge of the Maori Land Court; no longer does a majority of the Tribunal have to be Maori.

- ❖ *1989* Establishment of Treaty of Waitangi Policy Unit within Department of Justice; the Tribunal has the power to recommend the return of Crown forest lands; income from the Crown Forestry Rental Trust is available for researching Treaty claims.

- ❖ *1992* The Tribunal cannot hear claims on commercial fishing (Fisheries Claims have been settled with the Sealord Deal).

- ❖ *1993* The Tribunal cannot recommend the return of private land.

- ❖ *1994* The Fiscal Envelope imposes a financial limit on total settlements ($1 billion spread over 10 years).

- ❖ *1995* Office of Treaty Settlements established.

- ❖ *1996* End of Fiscal Envelope but existing settlements are benchmarks for future settlements (e.g. Tainui set at 17 percent of total amount paid).

- ❖ *1998* Tribunal uses its power for the first time to order the return of former SOE land in the Turangi Township Remedies Report.

Settlements

- Waitomo 1989: Land at Waitomo Caves transferred subject to a lease, and loan of $1 million provided
- Commercial Fisheries 1992: $170,000,000
- Ngati Rangiteaorere 1993: $760,000
- Hauai 1993: $715,682
- Ngati Whakaue 1994: $5,210,000
- Waikato/Tainui raupatu 1995: $170,000,000
- Waimakuku 1995: $375,000
- Rotoma 1996: $43,931
- Te Maunga 1996: $129,032
- Ngai Tahu 1997: $170,000,000
- Ngati Turangitukua 1998: $5,000,000

Settlements have been concluded with Ngati Tama, Ngati Ruanui and some Taranaki claimants. In addition there have been several part-settlements. Settlements aim at removing the sense of grievance with a fair, comprehensive, final and durable solution. They typically involve a formal apology, a cash and asset settlement, cultural redress such as return of wahi tapu (spiritually important sites), and recognition of the claimants' special and traditional relationship with the natural environment with lakes, rivers, mountains, forests and wetlands, sometimes giving them more chances to share in management and decisions affecting these areas. Sometimes commercial property is also made available for a settlement. Progress on negiotiating settlements has been slow — generally at the rate of one per year. Priority has been given to raupatu (confiscation) settlements.

General comments

The Waitangi Tribunal was the first formal mechanism provided for Maori to seek redress. From a quiet beginning, it has grown in importance. After the 1983 Motunui Case it was clear that the Tribunal could influence government. It has earned a reputation for sound judgement and reasoned argument. The Principles underlying the settlements emphasise partnership and co-operation. The Tribunal has taken on a massive job of reviewing all of our past and in the process has built up a lot of information about our national history.

Long-standing grievances have been addressed in very practical ways. Since 1985 the Tribunal has produced over 30 major reports and an equal number of unpublished reports on smaller local problems. These reports have outlined the case for redress of grievances in a range of Maori claims on land, fishing, Maori language and other issues, and have frequently led to major shifts in policy. Iwi authority has been recognised and restored. All areas of public policy now have to include Maori perspectives, while a number of major laws of the land now require formal recognition of the Principles of the Treaty of Waitangi.

The cost

The claimants and the Tribunal have been very moderate in not asking for everything back. They ask for enough to give the tribe a base on which it can build. The costs so far have not been unmanageable. It amounts to about 0.3% of total annual government spending and about 0.1% of GDP. Everyone benefits from the increased productivity and lower social costs from Maori unemployment and dependency.

Criticisms

However, critics have commented adversely on time delays and costs. The Tribunal is underresourced and under pressure to hurry the process of finalising historical claims. Some claimant groups are divided and have problems agreeing to a settlement. The tribes or claimants further down the queue from those who have settled their claims may not be fairly treated if the money runs out before their grievances are considered.

Others criticise the growth of the Tribunal and its employment of researchers and lawyers, referring to it as a 'gravy train'. There are calls for greater transparency in the process of settling claims and more public debate on the Principles. One historian has commented that research findings sometimes treat complex situations too simplistically. Other commentators have said that the past is being judged by the values of the present. But in spite of all the criticism, the Tribunal is undoubtedly making a significant contribution to New Zealand society. As Alan Ward has said:

> . . . the political compact of 1840 has been reaffirmed, and the process of acknowledging and addressing demonstrated grievances arising from Treaty breaches is under way . . .
> [*An Unsettled History*, p. 167]

Key Points

❖ Revived interest in Waitangi Day was the first step in getting the Treaty recognised legally.

❖ The Waitangi Tribunal was set up as government began showing greater responsiveness to Maori aspirations.

❖ Principles for settling historical claims were established by the Crown.

- The Tribunal follows an inquiry rather than adversarial approach, with claims weighed against both Maori and English versions of the Treaty.
- In 1985 the Tribunal's jurisdiction was extended back from 1975 to the signing of the Treaty in 1840.

Further Reading

Waitangi Tribunal website: www.knowledgebasket.co.nz/waitangi

An Unsettled History: Treaty Claims in New Zealand Today by Alan Ward

Trick or Treaty? by Douglas Graham

Histories, Power and Loss: Uses of the Past — a New Zealand Commentary edited by Andrew Sharp and Paul McHugh

Chapter 8

Some Examples Of Tribunal Claims

Hawke

The very first claim was made by J. P. (Joe) Hawke and others of Ngati Whatua, after he had been discharged without conviction on a charge of taking shellfish. He claimed he had been prejudicially affected because

> he had a right under the Treaty to take shellfish.

In March 1978, the Tribunal reported to the effect that the claim was unsubstantiated and made no recommendation.

Manukau

A Manukau claim concerned

> a proposed thermal power station which would adversely affect Maori fishing grounds.

The Waitangi Tribunal Report of July 1985 agreed with the claimants but made no recommendation because the New Zealand Electricity Department decided not to proceed with the project.

Motunui

In 1982 the Te Ati Awa tribe of Taranaki claimed that

> the effluent from the Motunui synthetic fuels plant would pollute their traditional fishing grounds.

The claim got the support of environmentalists and some economists opposed to the development. The Tribunal agreed with the applicants, recommending to the Crown that the proposed ocean outfall for the Motunui plant be discontinued. At first Government reaction was somewhat cool, but when it became clear that the public was very concerned, a task force was set up. It considered development in the region and the issue of waste disposal. In 1986 the Government announced it would provide $11.7 million of the estimated $13 million to help build a new regional outfall at Motunui to dispose of waste left after land-based treatment. This successful claim renewed enthusiasm for recourse to the Waitangi Tribunal.

Kaituna

The Kaituna River claim, reported on by the Tribunal in November 1984, concerned

> a proposal to discharge Rotorua's sewage into the Kaituna River.

The Tribunal found in favour of the claimants. It recommended the Crown withdraw financial support for the disposal pipeline and divert it to a suitable land-disposal system. The recommendation was accepted by the Government and $21 million was spent on a new land-based waste plant for Rotorua.

> ### Spiritual values
> In the Kaituna River Report and the Manukau Report, the Tribunal emphasised Maori interests in waters not just for fishing, but in terms of spiritual values as well. Maori custom has strict rules about preparing and eating food. These rules originated from common sense and elementary hygiene. The rules are projected to a far-reaching degree. For example, it is unacceptable for anyone to sit on a table off which food is eaten. Water used for food preparation must be quite separate from water used for other purposes.
>
> The place where the discharge of sewage was planned in the Kaituna River was close to some burial caves and sacred places. It was near the clear, sparkling pool where one witness said his ancestors returning from battle would go to cleanse themselves of the tapu upon them after the bloodshed of war.
>
> For these reasons the Waitangi Tribunal decided that:
> *'To mingle the effluent with the waters of Lake Rotorua is offensive to Maori spiritual and cultural values.'*
> [From Kaituna River Report, 1984 Waitangi Tribunal, page 22]

Manukau Harbour

A further Manukau claim, lodged in May 1983, related

> to the despoliation of the Manukau harbour and loss of lands.

The Tribunal agreed that the tribes of the Manukau had been severely prejudiced in their enjoyment of traditional lands and fisheries. Compulsory acquisitions of land, industrial developments, reclamations, waste discharges, zonings, commercial fishing and denial of harbour access had all been contrary to the Treaty guarantees. The Tribunal recommended changes to the law and to Crown policy, along with an action plan — with participation by the tangata whenua — to clean up the harbour and restore its mana. They also recommended the return of certain lands and fisheries but

> rejected the idea of wholesale return of the harbour to Maori ownership as being unrealistic.

Not all these recommendations were acted on, although some progress was made. A Manukau Harbour Strategy was implemented and legislative change was embodied in the Resource Management Bill. However, the claimants remain far from satisfied.

Te Reo

> ### Maori language
> *Ka ngaro te reo, ka ngaro taua, pera i te ngaro o te moa*
> (Language without restorative measures would be as dead as the moa)
> As Sir James Henare made clear to the Waitangi Tribunal:
> *Ko te reo te mauri o te mana Maori* (The language is the core of our Maori culture and mana).

There were two distinctive features of this claim about te reo (the Maori language): it was for loss of cultural properties, rather than land or fisheries; and it was brought forward by an interest group on behalf of all Maori. The survival of the Maori language, fundamental to the culture and a key marker of cultural identity, was a growing cause of concern. In 1913, 90 percent of Maori schoolchildren could speak Maori. By 1953 this was down to 23 percent, and in 1975 fewer than 5 percent of Maori schoolchildren could speak Maori.

In May 1984, Huirangi Waikerepuru and Nga Kaiwhakapumau i te Reo (the Wellington Language Board) made a claim against the Crown for

> failing to protect Maori language. The claim alleged that government policies had contributed to the decline of te reo Maori, through neglect, and by actively forbidding Maori in schools and refusing to allow the use of Maori in court or in dealings with the Government.

The claimants' case was that te reo Maori should be recognised as an official language throughout New Zealand and for all purposes. The Maori Affairs Act 1953, the Broadcasting Act 1976, the Education Act 1964, the Health Act 1956, the Hospitals Act 1957 and various other broadcasting and educational policies were said to be inconsistent with the principles of the Treaty, and as a result the claimants were prejudiced in that they and other Maori were not able to have the Maori language spoken, heard, taught, learnt, broadcast or otherwise used for all purposes, and in particular in Parliament, the courts, government departments and local bodies and in all spheres of New Zealand society including hospitals. The Tribunal was told that no Maori was able to use te reo Maori in the courts if he or she could speak English.

> ### No Maori spoken in court
> *The 1979 High Court decision, confirmed in the Court of Appeal — Mihaka v. Police — was based on an English statute of 1362 which became part of New Zealand law in 1858. It had been designed to protect English natives against French-speaking Normans!*

The five recommendations made were based on the idea that the Maori language was a taonga:

1   Maori should be a lawful language in all courts of law

and in any dealings with government departments, local authorities and other public bodies.

2   A supervising body should be established by statute to supervise and foster the use of the Maori language.

3   There should be an inquiry into the way Maori children are educated, including the opportunity to learn te reo.

4   Broadcasting policy should recognise that the Treaty obliges the Crown to recognise and protect the Maori language.

5   Bilingualism should be a prerequisite for some appointments to state service.

The recommendations did not go as far as some claimants wished but did succeed in bringing about change in government policy. Some recommendations were not implemented; others were accepted but in a narrower framework. For example, no provision was made for Maori to be spoken in dealings with public authorities, and the provision for bilingualism was not accepted. But Maori language had finally received more recognition from the state.

The Maori Language Act 1987 declared Maori to be an official language of New Zealand and conferred the right to speak Maori in any legal proceedings, regardless of the ability to speak or understand in English or any other language.

A Maori Language Commission — Te Taura Whiri i te Reo Maori — was set up to actively promote Maori as a living language and to advise and assist the Crown on the implementation of Maori as an official language.

Concerns about the survival of the language also influenced a claim in 1990 about availability of radio frequencies.

Government policy was charged with not adequately providing for the promotion of Maori language and culture.

The Tribunal found that broadcasting was a vehicle for the protection of the Maori language and Maori should have access to airwave spectrums. It recommended a six-month suspension of the government tendering process and allocation of FM frequencies to Maori. After much argy-bargy in the courts (Court of Appeal, Privy Council) it was established that the Maori language was a taonga, was in a perilous state, and there was an obligation on the Crown to ensure te reo Maori had a proper place in broadcasting. But the Crown was not obliged to go beyond what was reasonable.

A new agency, Te Mangai Paho, was set up to promote Maori language and culture by making funds available for broadcasting and the production of programmes. It was financed by a proportion of the broadcasting fee and government funding for new projects. It was to promote a Maori television channel. After some delays and a few problems this hit our screens in early 2004.

Waiheke

Ngati Paoa of Waiheke, a landless tribe, lodged their claim in 1984. In June 1987 the Tribunal reported that in disposing of the Waiheke lands without inquiring into the position of the Ngati Paoa,

> the Crown, through the Board of Maori Affairs, had acted contrary to the Treaty.

Governor Hobson had been instructed in 1839 that Maori were to be protected from injuring themselves by selling land they might need for their future. This directive had been ignored. In early 1989 the Government restored the Waiheke Station to the Ngati Paoa as a going concern.

Meanwhile, an Amendment Act in 1985 extended the jurisdiction of the Tribunal to events occurring since the signing of the Treaty on 6 February 1840.

> *The nature of transaction*
> *The Waiheke Report of June 1987 was the first report to recommend returning land. It was the first one to suggest that the early land deals with the Ngati Paoa chiefs had been based on two different ideas about the nature of the transaction.*

Orakei-Bastion Point

The Orakei (Bastion Point) claim was the first one after the change to the extent of jurisdiction. The Tribunal found that

> the Crown, through acts and omissions contrary to the Treaty, had caused Ngati Whatua to become virtually landless.

The Bastion Point land had been the subject of an agreement between the elders, the Government and the Auckland City Council in 1979. Now the Tribunal recommended that more Crown land be returned and a tribal endowment made. The Crown accepted most of the Tribunal's recommendations in 1991.

> *A moderate solution*
> *This report was significant because the Tribunal did not consider full legal restitution for the value of the land lost (prime real estate in Auckland would have run into billions). Usually this would include the value of the property at the time of the loss plus compound interest. If full restitution was extended over all the claims present and future, the cost would be impossible. So the Tribunal opted for a moderate solution — what would the iwi need for their future?*

Te Roroa

In 1992 the Tribunal reported on the claims of the Te Roroa, a northern tribe who claimed they had been unfairly deprived of several large blocks of land. One of the local private farmers owned land, with a burial site, supposed to have been reserved for the tribe. He had bought it in good faith. There was a prolonged confrontation between local Maori and farmers.

The Tribunal Report recommended that the land be purchased by the Crown and returned to Te Roroa.

This created widespread concern about other possible claims over private land. The Crown eventually felt obliged to buy the land from the farmer and return it to the tribe. Some politicians and Federated Farmers wanted the Tribunal's powers reduced so that it could make no further recommendations about privately owned land.

> ### Private land
> The Government amended the Act to prevent the Tribunal from making recommendations over private land. The Tribunal has taken the firm position that it will not consider claims when the land is occupied or under threat of occupation.

Muriwhenua

In June 1985, the Muriwhenua people of the Far North lodged a wide-ranging claim relating to Crown control over their fisheries and various tracts of land. This was to prove a crucial claim, as it triggered off the whole fishing quota situation and a ruling by the Court of Appeal about State-Owned Enterprises (for more on this part of the claim see the next chapter).

The land claim and the Tribunal Report raised significant issues. One was whether the early land sales had been just — whether Maori had really understood to what extent the land was alienated from them by sale to Pakeha. If both parties to

Muriwhenua claim area, Northland, showing principal hapu and current marae

the transaction had quite different understandings of what they were agreeing to, was it a fair sale? The Tribunal Report said it was not. The Tribunal also found that

> the Government failed to investigate the pre-Treaty sales

— if sales they were — and

> that Government purchases were not fair and valid.

The Government had also

> failed to ensure that sufficient reserves were created for Maori.

The social consequences for the Muriwhenua were serious. They were marginalised on lands where even subsistence living was impossible. Muriwhenua have a higher unemployment rate than other Maori and on other socioeconomic indicators are slightly poorer than other Maori.

Professor Bill Oliver, an academic historian, questioned the conclusions of the Tribunal, seeing their conclusions as an oversimplification of a complex issue. Progress on the Muriwhenua claim has been bogged down by disagreements within the tribe.

The Tainui and Ngai Tahu settlements were major ones. They were relatively quickly settled because they already had a pan-tribal structure. There were not so many disagreements between hapu and iwi. The Minister in Charge of Treaty Settlements, Douglas Graham, played a decisive role in the negotiations.

Tainui (the Waikato part)
Waikato Raupatu Claims Settlement Act 1995

This claim, concluded in 1995, was the first major one settled. It was signed off by Te Arikinui Dame Te Atairangikaahu, the Maori Queen, and by Prime Minister Jim Bolger. Queen Elizabeth II signed off its passage through Parliament personally.

> ### Compensation for confiscation
> The claim concerned land confiscated by the 1863 New Zealand Settlements Act. These are known as raupatu lands, taken by force after the wars between British and colonial forces and the Waikato between 1859–63. Some compensation had already been paid after a commission in 1927 had found the actions of the troops and confiscation unwarranted. But no land had been returned. In 1991 the Labour Government offered Tainui a $9 million take-it-or-leave-it deal, but Tainui wanted land for land.

The settlement

> involved the return of 15,000 hectares, an apology to the
> Maori Queen and monetary compensation.

The total value was $170 million. It did not include the Tainui claims relating to the Waikato River and the Manukau, Raglan, Kawhia and Aotea harbours. It included guarantees to protect existing tenants such as the University of Waikato, and it set a benchmark for future claims in that it was seen as representing 17 percent of historical claims. In return, the Tainui agreed to withdraw their claims over coal and to accept the deal as full and final settlement in respect of confiscated land.

Tainui had to set up a new tribal corporate structure as a result of the settlement. The Tainui Maori Trust Board, which had negotiated, was not appropriate for the next stage. Not all Tainui were in favour of the settlement, though. Some, like activist Eva Rickard, felt the Tainui Maori Trust Board could not represent all hapu.

Whakatohea

The Whakatohea of Opotiki had opted for direct negotiation with the Crown. Their claim was about

> land confiscated after the murder/execution of missionary
> Reverend Carl Volkner in 1865.

Chief Mokomoko, blamed and executed for the deed because the perpetrator was out of reach, had received a Crown pardon, but the land was not returned.

The Draft Settlement, signed on 1 October 1996, included an apology for the invasion of Whakatohea lands, the wrongful labelling of the tribe as rebels and the subsequent confiscation, and a $40 million package with an immediate income for the tribe of $3.6 million a year. But interhapu rivalry stalled the negotiations and the Government offer was withdrawn in 1998 after the deadline passed. Now Whakatohea go to the back of the queue. Their experience shows the importance of tribes sorting out who speaks for them before negotiations begin.

Ngai Tahu

The Ngai Tahu Settlement was signed on 5 October 1996 by Sir Tipene O'Regan and Charlie Croft for Ngai Tahu, and the Minister in Charge of Treaty Settlements, Douglas Graham.

The settlement followed two years of hearings and a report by the Tribunal published in 1991. It involved $170 million in cash and land. It differed from the Tainui claim in that it did not deal with confiscated land. As with the Tainui, an earlier token settlement had been made.

> The Government had bought land at ridiculously low prices and failed to provide the promised reserves,

a condition of the sales.

> The Crown had failed to ensure the maintenance of an adequate economic base for Ngai Tahu.

Ngai Tahu was offered Crown properties at market prices and given title to farmable parts of the Elfin and Routeburn high-country stations. Title to non-farmable parts was based on an understanding that the land would be leased back to the Conservation Minister in perpetuity for a peppercorn rental. Codfish Island (Whenuahau) was to remain in Crown ownership and the Muttonbird Islands (Titi) would have Ngai Tahu title but would be managed as a nature reserve (but Ngai Tahu kept the traditional right to take muttonbirds). Raratoka Island was to have Ngai Tahu title, and the restoration of original Maori names for 78 places including Aoraki (Mt Cook) was guaranteed. Flexibility meant that Ngai Tahu could select Crown properties from an agreed list to value at no more than $200 million.

Media reaction was generally favourable but the Royal Forest and Bird Protection Society expressed worries over conservation issues. Ngai Tahu found the settlement (Sir Tipene O'Regan) 'acceptable but not fair'. There was some opposition from within the tribe, with the ancient Waitaha tribe and the Tuhuru hapu of the West Coast claiming their position had been compromised.

> ### Conservation compromise
> *This was a major and lengthy claim made in respect of land, sea fisheries and mahinga kai (traditional food sources). A small number of areas important for conservation have been returned to the tribe. Many places have been leased back to the Crown, some with co-management by Ngai Tahu. The settlement was a compromise between conservationist concerns and Maori determination to recover the mana and rangatiratanga over their lands.*

Tainui

The Taranaki Claim was based on the three ways they lost land:

> by confiscation, aggressive government land purchases, and dubious decisions from the Native Land Court.

This was a tribe that had suffered appalling losses. The Taranaki Report was released in June 1996.

> The Tribunal assessed their losses as the worst in the country.

Some hapu had lost everything. No hapu had had sufficient lands returned to provide even minimum relief. Even when some reserves were eventually defined, they were handed over to administrators rather than to the owners. Leases in perpetuity were then sold to settlers. All land was put in individual titles, even reserves, and those living away from Taranaki were excluded from ownership.

Negotiations soon got bogged down. A major problem is presented by the idea that all settlements should be full and final. The Tribunal's Report doubts that it will be able to do justice to the full extent of tribal suffering; the claim may be assessed in billions of dollars, but negotiations may be for a fraction of that sum. Other complications are that the Taranaki claim will be led by five or six groups, each with a mandate for certain hapu within Taranaki but without being able to represent others. There has never been a single pan-tribal structure in Taranaki, which makes negotiations difficult, and it will make for a more complex negotiating process.

Turangi

The Turangi Claim was all about

> land taken under the Public Works Act in the 1960s for hydroelectricity and the Turangi township.

The claim, by the Turangitukua hapu, had been lodged in 1988 and the Report was completed in 1995. It was a test case because the land not needed for hydroelectricity or the township had been on-sold but with memorials on the titles after the State-Owned Enterprises Act of 1986 and the successful appeal by the Maori Council. This was the first time the Tribunal exercised its power to order the return of such land. It ordered the return of commercial land but not residential land and the return of Crown-owned properties. Cash for the restoration of marae and wahi tapu and for a start fund for Maori enterprises was also involved.

River claims

Claims involving tino rangatiratanga over rivers, such as the Mohaka River claim, the Te Ika Whenua claim over rivers in the eastern Bay of Plenty, and the Whanganui River claim raise interesting issues. The Waitangi Tribunal accepted the evidence of the claimants and of two Maori Land Court judges that rivers were living indivisible entities, the taonga of the tribes that controlled and used them. These claims involve more than just a right of use and it was not clear whether these claims to 'ownership of the river' had been extinguished. But the Tribunal went on to consider that the Treaty implied an agreement to share resources, though that did not necessarily detract from tino rangatiratanga over the rivers.

> The Crown, in not protecting or compensating for their residual interests in the rivers had breached the principle of active protection.

However, in 1999 the Crown made an abrupt rejection of the Tribunal's argument that Maori had an interest in rivers akin to ownership. That they had a special interest the Crown agreed, and said this would be taken into account in negotiations. Clearly the whole concept of ownership, different types of ownership, and owning interests in a river will be explored more fully in the future.

Key Points

- ❖ Raupatu claims concerned land confiscated after the wars.
- ❖ The Muriwhenua claim raised issues about State-owned land being sold to private owners before claims had been settled, and about the fishing claims of all the tribes.
- ❖ Claims are settled more easily when a pan-tribal structure such as that of Ngai Tahu already exists.
- ❖ The Tribunal does not ask for complete restitution.

❖ Compensation is based on what the tribe needs in order to build its own economic independence.

❖ Cultural claims concern issues such as the loss of the Maori language and its implications.

Further Reading

An Unsettled History: Treaty Claims in New Zealand Today by Alan Ward

Waitangi Tribunal Reports

The Waitangi Tribunal website: www.waitangi-tribunal.govt.nz

Chapter 9

Fisheries and the Treaty

Competition for the fishing resources of New Zealand highlighted many of the main issues about the Treaty of Waitangi.

Early Maori fishing practices

The first Europeans found the extent of Maori fishing surprising and impressive. Joseph Banks, botanist on the *Endeavour*, described a net measuring 700–900 metres. In 1814, L. J. Nicholls stated: 'their nets are much larger than any that are made use of in Europe'. In one operation described by R. H. Mathews in 1855, over 7000 sharks were caught — 265 on one canoe alone. Fish were traded with other tribes. Fishing sites, up to 25 miles out to sea, were named and identified. Each fishing ground, located by cross-bearings from land, was associated with a particular type of fish and season. The Muriwhenua were fishing inshore (12 miles) from land and beyond. One fishing ground was located 48 miles from shore.

Clearly fishing was very important to the Maori economy. The fishing grounds were owned by different tribes and shared out between hapu. Fishing was necessary for survival and was an essential element of trade with other tribes and later with settlers. Maori trade took the form of delayed reciprocal payments. The missionary William Colenso noted in 1868:

> Dried sea-fish, or dried edible sea-weed, or shark oil, or karaka berries, would be given by natives living on the sea coast to friendly tribes dwelling inland; who would afterwards repay with potted birds, or eels, or hinau cakes or mats . . .

Muriwhenua fisheries claim

In May 1988 the Tribunal presented a report on the Muriwhenua fisheries claim, showing that before the Treaty they were extensively involved in fishing for domestic and commercial purposes, and how laws from the 1880s up to 1986 progressively robbed the Muriwhenua of their fishing rights (guaranteed by Article 2 of the Treaty). The findings of the Tribunal were crucial in the fisheries negotiations, playing a major role in reversing the Crown's appreciation of the extent of Maori fishing rights.

The Treaty of Waitangi

The English version guaranteed Maori 'full and exclusive and undisturbed possession of their Lands and Estates Forests Fisheries and other properties'. The Maori text was less specific, using the word 'taonga', meaning precious treasures. Certainly fishing would have been among the most valued of their resources, as the English text recognised.

As settlement expanded so did competition over fish resources. Maori fishing rights were whittled away, especially when they lost land. Eel weirs and inland fisheries were no longer accessible. There were complaints at the Orakei Conference in 1879 about Pakeha trespassing on foreshores, restrictions on taking shellfish, and the loss of specific areas like pipi beds in the Manukau Harbour. The Treaty's fishery guarantee had been undermined, and the fisheries had been effectively taken away.

By 1866, Maori fishing rights were interpreted very narrowly.

Their rights were confined to their own consumption and not commercial development. For example, the Oyster Fisheries Act 1866, the first fish law in New Zealand, which provided for the leasing of oyster beds for commercial purposes, made no specific provisions for Maori apart from not allowing them to sell oysters from their own reserves. The Fish Protection Act 1877, the first comprehensive fisheries control measure, recognised the Treaty and made brief recognition of Maori rights. The Sea Fisheries Act 1884 omitted the Treaty altogether, while again the sale of oysters from beds reserved for Maori was forbidden. So the legislation made only a token acknowledgement of Maori fishing rights at most.

By the 1960s and 1970s it was clear that the inshore fisheries were being seriously overfished and some sort of management and conservation system was necessary.

The Government begins the quota system

In the early 1980s the government set up a system of managing and conserving the resource. (Fisheries Act 1983) They assumed that, as in the past, Maori rights only covered personal needs such as gathering shellfish for the family or small-scale catches of fin fish for customary purposes. These were all basically non-commercial activities.

A quota system was introduced. Fishermen were to buy a quota from the Crown, which gave them the right to catch the total amount of any species in a particular area. Quotas could be traded by sale, lease or licence. No provision was made for customary fisheries. Small-scale or part-time fishermen were disadvantaged and many lost their licences. The impact of the quota system was equally serious for many part-time Maori fishermen in the North.

The role of the Waitangi Tribunal

In December 1986 the Waitangi Tribunal warned the Ministry

of Agriculture and Fisheries that the quota system was inconsistent with the Treaty of Waitangi as it did not take into account Maori fishing rights. It was also in direct conflict with evidence being presented to the Waitangi Tribunal by Ngai Tahu and the various iwi of Muriwhenua of pre-existing and unextinguished collective tribal fishing rights which were protected by section 88(2) of the Fisheries Act 1983. Representatives of four Maori groups — Ngai Tahu, Muriwhenua, Tainui and the New Zealand Maori Council — sought and won an injunction on behalf of iwi in 1987. This stopped the Crown from allocating further quotas until Maori fishing rights had been clarified.

Meanwhile, Waitangi Tribunal reports were working on the details. The Tribunal found that the Treaty of Waitangi guaranteed to Maori full, exclusive and undisturbed possession of their fisheries, that iwi and hapu held collective fishing rights in the waters adjacent to their rohe (area of control) and that such rights included the right to use new technology to develop commercial fishing in New Zealand waters.

In addition, a Law Commission Report on Maori Fishing Rights of 1989 acknowledged that neither the law nor past government policies gave adequate recognition to Maori interests in fisheries, especially sea fisheries. The Commission noted that governments have tended to decide claims on the basis of English rules, principles and priorities without giving Maori views full weight.

Negotiation

An interim settlement involved a two-year adjournment of the fisheries litigation in return for a phased delivery of 10 percent of the Total Allowable Commercial Catch for each fish stock of each species in the Quota Management System. It also included $10 million in cash to a Maori Fisheries Commission and the establishment of Aotearoa Fisheries Ltd. These assets, together with further quotas and other assets acquired in the market, were later to become known as the Pre-Settlement Assets.

By 1992 the Maori Fisheries Commission held some 11 percent of the total quota and had acquired control of the nation's largest specialist inshore fishing business, Moana Pacific Fisheries Ltd. This was a commercial company wholly owned by the Commission. The proceeds were to be used for Maori social and economic development. The other half of the 10 percent quota was to be made available for lease to Maori fishermen. Maori were not enthusiastic about this deal, because it fell far short of the 50 percent they had claimed and the Maori Fisheries Commission was seen as an unnecessary compromise of individual tribal rights.

The Sealord deal

The Sealord Products Company held 26 percent of the total quota for New Zealand. When it came up for sale it was a unique opportunity. Maori wanted to buy all the company and quota, but the final deal was to buy half — and partner Brierley Investments Ltd bought the other half. The Deal of Settlement was signed on 23 September 1992.

Details

- The Crown paid $150 million in three sums of $50 million. The first instalment was to help the Commission to buy a half-share in Sealord Products in a joint venture.

- Twenty percent of new species brought into the Quota Management System was to be handed to the Commission for the benefit of all Maori.

- The Maori Fisheries Commission was restructured into a more representative body called the Treaty of Waitangi Fisheries Commission, Te Ohu Kai Moana.

- A Deed of Settlement was drawn up providing for customary fisheries and Maori involvement in fisheries statutory bodies.

In return:
- That's it for commercial fishing claims for all Maori. All current and future claims of commercial fishing are settled.
- Other laws recognising Maori fishing rights were to be repealed.

Maori reaction

The Maori share of the total quota would be 37.5 percent. There were lots of hui (23 marae and two national) and there was general support for the deal. However, concerns were expressed about protecting traditional fishing rights, and inland tribes were opposed to the inclusion of traditional and freshwater fish. It bothered some that they couldn't look too carefully at the deal because it was commercially sensitive. Some Maori leaders were vigorously opposed to removal of Treaty rights. To some, the Sealord Deal signalled a departure from legally based Treaty arguments for the settlement of Maori claims. They had to balance practical economic considerations against more lofty Treaty principles. The Waitangi Tribunal considered that it was wrong to extinguish Treaty-based Maori fishing rights, that it would have been more reasonable to have a 25-year moratorium, but gave their support to the deal in the end.

Both the Crown and the Waitangi Tribunal considered there was enough support to go ahead and sign a formal deal. These assets are generally referred to as the Post-Settlement Assets. The Deed, commonly called the Sealord Deal, was given effect by the enactment of the Treaty of Waitangi (Fisheries Claims) Settlement Act 1992.

Customary fishing rights

Maori negotiators were adamant that customary non-commercial fishing rights should be preserved, and these rights have been upheld by the courts.

> ### Court decisions
> In January 1984 a Maori fisherman, Tom Te Weehi, received a District Court conviction for taking undersize paua. This conviction was quashed by the High Court. Mr Justice Williamson upheld traditional Maori fishing rights based on custom. He held that Section 88(2) of the Fisheries Act 1983, which stated 'Nothing in this Act shall affect any Maori fishing rights', was limited to Ngai Tahu for personal food.
>
> In 1997, Kirk McRitchie of Ngati Hine, Ngati Ruawai, Ngati Waikarapu hapu was fishing for trout in Mangawhero River without a licence. The prosecution was dismissed even though trout is an introduced species. The Judge said the focus is on the fisheries rather than species and McRitchie was exercising a customary Maori fishing right.

A joint Maori and Crown Customary Fisheries Working Party produced a set of regulations including:
- Exclusive control of mataitai reserves (traditional fisheries providing food for domestic consumption) by the adjacent hapu or marae ;

- Kaitiaki (guardians) would manage the reserves;

- Honorary officers to be appointed to protect and enforce customary fishing rights.

Before a mataitai reserve (an area where local Maori have exclusive fishing rights) is established, a number of conditions must be met — for example, ensuring that it does not interfere with commercial quotas or non-commercial local fishing.

Together with existing legislation, the Treaty of Waitangi (Fisheries Claim) Settlement Act 1992 enables the establishment of fishing reserves and recognises the rights of iwi to manage them.

Ngai Tahu fishing claim

The second part of this claim concerned fisheries. The Tribunal found that Ngai Tahu were prejudicially affected by various acts and omissions, policies and statutes of the Crown relating to their sea fisheries and that this was inconsistent with the Treaty of Waitangi. The Tribunal criticised the effect of the Quota Management Scheme on Ngai Tahu Treaty rights and found that Ngai Tahu had an exclusive Treaty right to sea fisheries surrounding the whole of their coastline to 12 miles or so, but not 100 percent of all sea fisheries off their boundaries. This caused great panic in the media, who confused the findings with the recommendations, but the Tribunal did not recommend that most of the South Island fisheries be handed over to Ngai Tahu or that all fisheries within 12 miles of the coast be returned to them.

Instead, the recommendation was that the negotiated settlement should include an additional percentage of quota to Ngai Tahu. In the non-commercial area the recommendation involved the return of exclusive eel-fishing rights in Te Waihora (Lake Ellesmere) and certain mahinga kai reserves (food resources).

Allocating the quota

The Sealord Deal was for all Maori, including those who did not sign the agreement and also inland tribes. One crucial issue was how to determine who got what. Was it to be determined on coastline ownership, or population of the tribe, or the tribe's dependency on fishing? Were urban Maori entitled to a share?

Coastline ownership would give Ngai Tahu an advantage over tribes like the Muriwhenua with a smaller coastline but more people. For example, Ngai Tahu with 22,269 people would receive about $4533 per person whereas Muriwhenua with 18,492 people would receive $204 per person. A Treaty Tribes Coalition was formed to lobby for the coastline model (Ngai Tahu, Hauraki, Ngai Tamanuhiri, Ngati Tama, Ngati Kahungunu). Heated arguments ensued.

What does it mean?

population-based distribution = mana totoru o te tangata
coastline = mana whenua mana moana

Two large urban authorities in Auckland — Te Whanau o Waipareira and Manukau Urban Maori Authority — lodged a claim with Waitangi Tribunal on behalf of urban Maori, many of whom had lost connections with their tribal base. This claim was opposed by Ngai Tahu and their allies. After many legal battles a special fund called the Putea Trust was to be set up for all Maori, including those who had lost touch with their iwi.

In 1997 the Commission announced the allocation plan. The method of allocating was called Ahu Whakamua:

- Inshore quotas to be allocated to iwi on the basis of actual tribal coastline. (Inshore quota = fish-stocks caught at depths down to 300 metres.)

- Deepwater quotas to be 75% iwi population, 25% iwi coastline. (Deepwater = fish caught at depths greater than 300 metres.)

- Cash to be allocated to iwi using a population formula.

- Also funds set aside for all Maori, particularly those who cannot find or do not associate with their iwi.

The Putea Trust, a $20-million fund, was to be established, with all Maori eligible to apply for assistance from this fund.

- Freshwater Fisheries Fund established.

- Creation of the largest fishing company in New Zealand, Aotearoa Fisheries Limited, which would issue 'income shares' to all iwi on a population basis. (It has to pay out 40% of net profit after tax to owners of income shares.)

- In early 2003 the Commission was to report to the Ministry of Fisheries to allow for allocation to begin.

- Separate proposal for the Chatham Islands — a special fishery zone of inshore and deepwater fisheries with the assets going to Chatham Islands iwi.

> **What's your iwi**
> 1991 census: 22% of Maori did not know the name of their iwi
>
> 1996 census: 19% still unable to identify their iwi

The result

Te Ohu Kai Moana has become a major stakeholder in the fishing industry with assets totalling over $700 million in 2002. The assets are growing at 8.8% per year compounding. There is active promotion of Maori involvement in the fishing industry through educational programmes and quota-leasing arrangements. By 1996, $1 million was budgeted for scholarships. In 2002, $10 million was allocated for a fisheries development fund, including research for customary, marine, aquaculture and freshwater fisheries. By and large, fishing ventures have been profitable and most iwi have reinvested profits back into the industry as well as used them for a wide range of customary and social purposes including marae, health, education and language.

Key Points

- ❖ Fishing has always been an important resource for Maori.
- ❖ Rights guaranteed by the Treaty were whittled away.
- ❖ Introducing the quota system for all New Zealand fishermen (1983) brought the issue into the open.
- ❖ After the Sealord Deal (1992), all Maori have a share in 37.5 percent of the total quota.
- ❖ Customary fishing rights (non-commercial) give specific rights to specific hapu.

Further Reading

Te Ohu Kai Moana: The Treaty of Waitangi Fisheries Commission — www.tokm.co.nz

The Waitangi Tribunal (1988) Muriwhenua Fishing Report (see pages 68–74, and 37–44) and the Ngai Tahu Report

Chapter 10

The Treaty, the Lawyers and the Politicians

Who makes the decisions about the Treaty?

We inherited a form of government from Great Britain called the Westminster System. Parliament, elected by the people (whether by First Past the Post or MMP) is the highest court in the land. Only Parliament can make the law. The task of the law courts is to *interpret* the law.

This was the system which had evolved over centuries in Great Britain before it was imported into New Zealand. It ignores Maori political structures and the special status of Maori and the Treaty of Waitangi. However, contemporary considerations about the constitutional status of the Treaty of Waitangi are now entering the mix. These see the Treaty as a contract against which the Crown's treatment has to be

> **Government**
> *There are three branches of government:*
>
> **the Executive** — *Monarch/Governor-General, Cabinet and Prime Minister, responsible for administering the laws;*
>
> **the Legislature** — *Parliament which makes the law; and*
>
> **the Judiciary** — *the law courts which interpret the law.*

assessed. Exploring the constitutional issues has kept the courts and the politicians jostling one another for dominance.

The President of the Court of Appeal, Sir Robin Cooke, when making a judgment on the Tainui claim, commented that: '. . . in the end no doubt only the courts can finally rule on whether or not a particular solution accords with the Treaty principles.' This comment led the Prime Minister in December 1989 to state the Government's position on constitutional matters relating to the Treaty. The Prime Minister (Geoffrey Palmer, later Sir Geoffrey Palmer) said the Government accepted that the Court of Appeal in the Tainui case had correctly decided the actual points of law before it. However, he said, the President's comment quoted above raised important constitutional issues. In a paper entitled 'Constitutional Matters Raised by Treaty of Waitangi Issues', the Prime Minister said that all three branches of government — Parliament, the courts, and the executive — had in recent years played a significant role in addressing Maori grievances under the Treaty. But he said it would be of concern if the comment of the President of the Court of Appeal 'were to indicate the readiness of that or any other court to move outside of what is seen as its traditional role of interpreting, explaining and thus developing the law'.

Geoffrey Palmer said that any such move would suggest that the courts had the power to contradict Parliament, which would seriously damage the constitutional balance of power between the three branches of government. The issues arising from the Treaty were, he said, a matter of major social policy with important economic and racial implications. Parliament's role as the ultimate arbiter of such issues could not be ousted. The Government will make the final decisions on them, he declared.

But in 1995, Sian Elias (later Chief Justice from 2000) argued that the Treaty contained promises made by the Crown to Maori and that the transfer of sovereignty was conditional on those promises being kept. She also considered that the

Treaty promises were ongoing, not a one-off situation.

In 1999, Justice E. W. Thomas in the Court of Appeal expressed a view that the Treaty of Waitangi was a constitutional limitation on the legislative power. This implied limits on the sovereignty of Parliament. The basis of constitutional authority, he claimed, was the consent of the governed and in the case of the Maori, their conditional consent under the Treaty. This line of interpretation would bring us closer to the American system of judicial review of laws.

A partnership of Parliament and the Courts

Both the courts and Parliament have contributed to clarifying the issues. Some government policy came about not by design but because of court rulings. For example, the policy to recognise Maori interests in surplus Crown properties arose only because of a Court of Appeal ruling after the New Zealand Maori Council challenged the Crown over the State-Owned Enterprises Act 1987. The current seabed and foreshore debate is another example where government policy follows a court ruling. The Waitangi Tribunal itself can only make *recommendations* to government (except where the Tribunal may *order* the repurchase of land sold by State-Owned Enterprises if it is required to settle land claims).

Recent Government policy and the Treaty

After the 1984 election, the Labour Government included the Treaty in several laws and in the terms of reference for the Royal Commission on Social Policy. A Cabinet Minute of March 1986 required government departments to recognise the Treaty in all aspects of department administration and in the preparation of all legislation. The Treaty was to be treated as if it were part of domestic law. It was to apply to all policies. Maori were to be consulted on all matters relating to its application.

That stance was revised in June 1986, the reference to the Treaty as domestic law was dropped, and the term 'Treaty' was qualified as 'Principles of the Treaty'. This approach went much further than any previous government had gone but was more a directive on processes than a fixed policy.

In 1988, the Government set out its policy in the document 'Partnership Perspectives He Tirohanga Rangapu'. In 1989 the Government decided on a pro-active stance and released its Treaty Principles (see Chapter 2). In more recent times, government policy on the foreshore and seabed has been proposed (see Chapter 11).

How the 1986 Directive affected new legislation
The directive stated:

> That all future legislation referred to Cabinet at the policy approval stage should draw attention to any implications for recognition of the Principles of the Treaty of Waitangi, that departments should consult with appropriate Maori people on all significant matters affecting the application of the Treaty, with the Minister of Maori Affairs to provide assistance if necessary.

It included a requirement to assess the financial and resource implications. Those preparing legislation must give priority to identifying Maori interests, and to consultation with the relevant community. Consultation was to be carried out in such a way that Maori people are comfortable, must be seen to have clear results and must include feedback to the Maori community. The Ministry of Maori Affairs was to play an important role by reviewing and commenting on all government activity where a Maori perspective was required.

Some statutes contain a Treaty clause — these are all linked to physical resources, such as land, the environment or Treaty settlements. The best known of these is the Resource Management Act 1991, which consolidated the 54 laws governing New Zealand's land, air and water resources.

Resource Management law

This legislation, introduced to Parliament in December 1989, made resource management the responsibility of regional and local government. It provided for the consideration of the Treaty of Waitangi and the concerns of Maori generally in all resource management matters.

The Resource Management Act 1991 states that:

> In achieving the purpose of this Act, all persons exercising functions and powers under it, in relation to managing the use, development, and protection of natural and physical resources, shall take into account the principles of the Treaty of Waitangi (Te Tiriti o Waitangi) . . .

The new law recognised the concept of kaitiakitanga as an integral part of sustainable management. Maori are able to continue to use geothermal energy for domestic, some therapeutic and other uses. Mining prospectors are required to have special regard for wahi tapu (special or sacred places) and to make reasonable attempts to consult with the owners of the land. It also recognised the interests of Maori in the coastal environment in the protection of wahi tapu, shellfish collection and areas where weaving materials are gathered.

What does it mean?

Kaitiakitanga is defined in the Act as the exercise of guardianship; and, in relationship to a resource, includes the ethic of stewardship based on the nature of the resource itself.

A kaitiaki is appointed by tribal kaumatua, kuia or tohunga (elders of the tribe). The person appointed is selected from the tangata whenua (local hapu). The position can be specific to one particular taonga such as fisheries or marae activities, and is accountable to the tribe. The position is part of the complex social, cultural, economic and spiritual system established through long tribal associations with land and water.

Local Government

As local government operates under delegated authority, it inherits central government obligations. The two important Treaty issues for local government are Maori representation and participation in decision-making. In practice, some councils in predominantly Maori areas have a representative number of Maori councillors. The Local Government Commission has just (as of April 2004) boosted the number of Maori seats from two to three for Environment Bay of Plenty. Total seats number 14. The Whakatane Mayor, not a supporter of separate representation, said if there was to be Maori representation, it was fairer to have a seat for each of the three iwi in the region. The Commission used the ratio of the Maori electoral population to the total population of the region, to come up with a formula. Some councils have no Maori representation, although the Resource Management Act does oblige local government to involve Maori in relevant decisions.

Tikanga Maori (Maori way of doing things)

The executive, judicial and legislative branches of government are increasingly required to develop an understanding of tikanga Maori and how to apply those tikanga. This is not restricted to Treaty settlements, the Waitangi Tribunal or the Maori Land Court. Areas like the administration of Maori land, Treaty claims, representation (where required to consult or negotiate with Maori, especially regarding resource management), and allocation of settlement resources all include this requirement. There is a special project working on the law of succession, because Maori have very different perspectives and also big tribal differences on this topic. In such areas as child welfare, where supervision of children at risk is now delegated to iwi authorities, the administrators need an understanding of tikanga Maori. Environmental management, which involves local government and central government by virtue of section 6(e) of the Resource Management Act, requires those with discretions under the Act to:

> recognise and provide for . . . the relationship of Maori and their culture and traditions with their ancestral lands, water, sites, waahi tapu and other taonga.

All of these responsibilities require familiarity with tikanga Maori.

What does it mean?
Tika = that which is fair, true, just or a proper line of action. This is the origin of tikanga. It refers to the rules, customs and habits of Maori culture.

More about the partnership directives
These were to:
- honour the Principles of the Treaty through exercising powers reasonably and in good faith so as to actively protect Maori interests specified in the Treaty;
- eliminate the gaps — educational, personal, social, economic and cultural — between Maori and the general population that disadvantage Maori and do not result from individual or cultural preferences;
- provide opportunities for Maori to develop economic

activities so they achieve self-sufficiency, and eliminate attitudes of dependency;
- deal fairly, justly and expeditiously with breaches and grievances between the Crown and Maori;
- provide for Maori language and culture to receive an equitable allocation of resources;
- promote decision-making in the machinery of government, in areas of importance to Maori communities, allowing for participation on jointly agreed terms;
- encourage Maori participation in the political process.

Iwi as the delivery agent

Strengthening of the iwi and helping to restore their independence is a cornerstone of the government's approach. Those who signed the original Treaty did so as representatives of a specific iwi or hapu. Successive governments have considered the iwi the most appropriate organisation through which to deliver government programmes to the Maori people. They are seen as incorporating tradition, and as strong, enduring systems of co-operation and community effort.

What does it mean?

Iwi = a group descended from a common founding ancestor. Each iwi includes a number of hapu (subtribes). Each hapu consists of related whanau or family groups. Iwi have an identifiable and historical base. The boundaries are known to the group and on the whole were identified by the Maori Land Court in the 19th century. Every Maori person is born with one or a number of iwi affiliations.

But there is some debate about the role of iwi. Some are more effective than others, and skills and resources are unevenly distributed between them. Some iwi already well established may disadvantage others less developed and less able to promote their interests.

Key Points

- Both Parliament and the Law Courts have contributed to the development of our laws regarding the Treaty of Waitangi.

- The Treaty plays a crucial role in several of our most important laws, such as the Resource Management Act (1991).

- Understanding tikanga Maori, the Maori way of doing things, is increasingly important in our society.

- Because Government prefers to work through iwi organisations to deliver programmes to Maori, iwi authorities have become more important than in the past.

Further Reading

'A History of Crown Sovereignty in New Zealand' by Paul McHugh, in *Histories, Power and Loss: Uses of the Past — A New Zealand Commentary*, edited by Andrew Sharpe and Paul McHugh

The Treaty Now by William Renwick

An Unsettled History: Treaty Claims in New Zealand Today by Alan Ward

Chapter 11

Seabed and Foreshore

What does it mean?

Foreshore = the part of the beach that gets wet; the area between the low-tide mark and the point reached by the highest spring tide.

Seabed = the area under the sea, beyond the low-water mark.

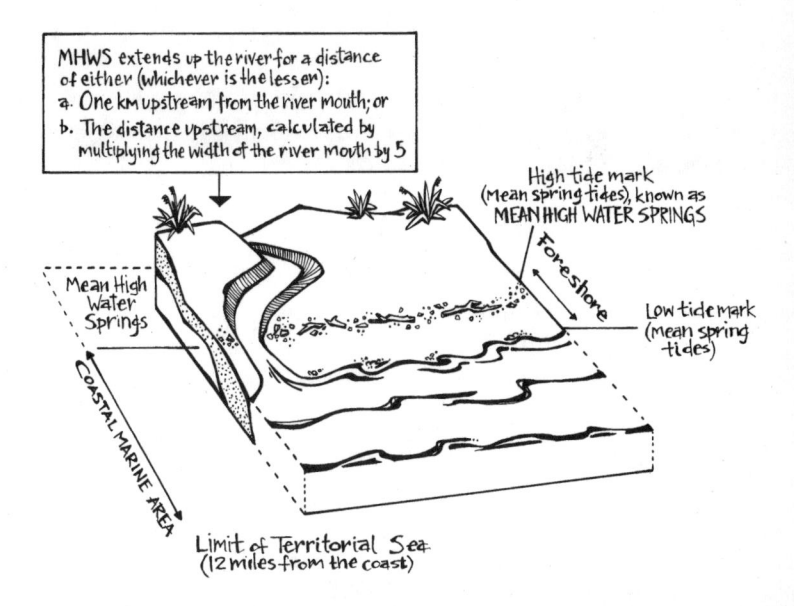

MHWS extends up the river for a distance of either (whichever is the lesser):
a. One km upstream from the river mouth; or
b. The distance upstream, calculated by multiplying the width of the river mouth by 5

High-tide mark (mean spring tides), known as MEAN HIGH WATER SPRINGS

Foreshore

Low tide mark (mean spring tides)

Mean High Water Springs

COASTAL MARINE AREA

Limit of Territorial Sea (12 miles from the coast)

Queen's Chain = the area inland of the high-water mark. This marginal strip is often, not always, owned by the Crown and is not affected by the new proposals.

Blue Water Title = under the Resource Management Act, when land is subdivided, any privately owned foreshore and seabed are transferred to public ownership. An esplanade reserve is then created. This has progressively reversed private titles created in the past.

What are the main issues?

Many Maori have believed their relationship with their patch of foreshore and seabed is akin to an ownership relationship and that the Court of Appeal has recognised what they have always known. Many Pakeha believed otherwise and were hugely surprised by the decision of the Court of Appeal. The passion of belief in each side shocked the other.

The issue doesn't originate from the Treaty of Waitangi but from customary title. Treaty claims to the Waitangi Tribunal arise when Maori have been prejudiced by an act or omission of the Crown and redress is sought. Aboriginal rights claims are not Treaty claims but rather

claims for recognition of customary rights through the Maori Land Court.

In the case of the foreshore and seabed, iwi and hapu are claiming not that the Crown has taken away the rights to the foreshore and seabed but that those rights still exist and must be recognised.

There is broad agreement that Maori have some ownership rights in the coastal environment, but different views especially as to how much and how the whole issue should be resolved. Maori want not just to be able to use the foreshore and seabed as they have done for hundreds of years but also to have development rights. This could enable an iwi or hapu which established a title to a piece of foreshore or seabed to

> ### Who owns the land next to the foreshore?
> New Zealand has a coastline of 19,883 kilometres (including the Chathams and Pitt Islands)
>
> **The Crown** — owns 37.64 percent of the coastline distance (7455 km) as National Parks, strips reserved from sale, and reserves for wildlife, heritage and railways.
>
> **Territorial authorities** — own 31.42% of the coastline distance (6239 km), in esplanade reserves, public recreation reserves and roads.
>
> 30.4 percent of the coastline distance (6,032 km) is in **private ownership**, down to the high-water mark. About a third of this is Maori land, covering a coastline of 2053 km.
>
> ### Is there existing private ownership of foreshore and seabed?
> There is some private ownership of foreshore and seabed.
> 1. Sometimes land has been eroded, partially or fully. There are 208 such parcels that began as dry land and are now totally eroded. Another 1000 parcels are partially eroded. Of the totally eroded areas, 0.4 km is Maori-owned, 43.8 km is general land. Of the partially eroded areas, 220 km is Maori land, 450 km is general land. An estimated further 670 km of coastline is suffering some erosion.
>
> 2. Some surveys have been done to below the mean high-water mark. (6.4 km of the coastline). Eleven such parcels are general land (1.4 km) and five such parcels are Maori owned (5 km).

commercially exploit resources such as sand, minerals or biological resources. The customary rights of indigenous peoples are recognised internationally, but New Zealand has never defined them.

How did the whole thing start?

It began over the allocation of marine-farming water space in the Marlborough Sounds. In the early 1990s marine farming in the Sounds was taking off. But competition for water space was becoming a critical issue and local iwi felt locked out. They had completely failed in their attempt to oppose applications for marine farming on customary grounds, and also found all their own resource consent applications turned down flat. The final straw was the decision by the Crown to impose a moratorium on marine farming applications in the Marlborough Sounds. The intention was to impose a coastal tendering system for marine farming, similar to the quota management system for fishing. It would have led to privatisation of large areas of coastal space within the Sounds.

Eight Marlborough iwi — Te Tau Ihu — took the case to the Court of Appeal (the Ngati Apa case). The main issue was:

> Can the Maori Land Court issue a seabed and foreshore title like those awarded for land but subject to caveats protecting public access and preventing sale?

Not a new issue

The issue has been around in some form or another since the signing of the Treaty. Legislation such as the Harbours Acts 1878 and 1950 and the Maori Affairs Act 1953 prevented the Native Land Court (now known as the Maori Land Court) from investigating these rights. Maori had no legal mechanism to have customary rights recognised in the foreshore and seabed until the repeal of those Acts (1991 and 1993) and the enactment of the Te Ture Whenua Maori Act 1993.

What the Court of Appeal decided

The Court of Appeal ruled in on 20 June 2003, some six or seven years after the application was filed, that Maori could take a case to the Maori Land Court for determining customary title over parts of the foreshore and seabed, which then had the potential to be converted to a freehold title.

All the judges agreed that the Maori Land Court did have the jurisdiction to determine the status of the foreshore and seabed; it was not restricted to dry land. They agreed that New Zealand common law was different from English common law and that the Crown acquiring sovereignty was not the same as owning everything. Therefore, Maori property rights, when proven, had to be respected and given effect to (Chief Justice Elias was very clear on this point).

What was the reaction?

A landmark decision, said the lawyers. The politicians and the public panic: *have we lost our right to have a barbecue at the beach?*

The Government proposes preventing the Maori Land Court from awarding a freehold title to the foreshore and seabed. It wants to exclude the potential for findings which could establish property rights.

Maori groups have differing views: some say due legal process should be followed; others want the role of the kaitiaki of the seabed and foreshores recognised; some see co-management, others exclusive rights. All are concerned about protecting cultural and spiritual sites and practice and the coastal marine environment.

Customary rights

When did customary rights begin?

Some time after Mexico and Peru were colonised in the 16th and 17th centuries, the Spanish Crown came to accept that it had an obligation to protect the property rights of indigenous peoples. That obligation developed into the doctrine of aboriginal title. It became part of English common law, and by the time the Treaty of Waitangi was signed, the British Colonial Office accepted it too. The guarantees of article two of the Treaty are very close to a restatement of these obligations.

Shortly after the signing of the Treaty, the Crown realised that all parts of New Zealand were owned by Maori according to custom. Agreement would be necessary before the Crown could acquire land to on-sell to settlers. The Native Land Court (1862) was set up to translate customary title into a legally recognised title. This would make it easier for the Crown to transfer ownership to Pakeha.

Exactly what are customary rights?

There are different opinions about what a customary right involves. Some say that to claim a customary right the resource has to have been in continuous use. Some say it gives the right to develop a resource commercially. Others say it does not. The New Zealand Government view is that New Zealand law is not well developed in this area. They point out that courts in other countries apply certain tests. For example:

- Whether the interest or activity is an element of the practice, custom or tradition integral to the distinctive group claiming the right;

- Whether the interest or activity was being undertaken at the time of the signing of the treaty and continues to be undertaken;

- Whether the customary right has been extinguished by or under some other law.

This is a very narrow interpretation of customary rights and very different from that claimed by groups such as Te Ope Mana a Tai. They say that under current law in New Zealand none of these three elements are required to be demonstrated. According to Te Ope Mana a Tai, by quoting the very restrictive test adopted in Australia, the Crown is trying to restrict the scope and ability of the tangata whenua to prove their customary rights. Te Ope Mana a Tai question whether this is an appropriate approach for New Zealand.

> ### Te Ope Mana a Tai
> This is an interest group of iwi representatives concerned about the seabed and foreshore issue. They hope for the creation of titles protecting public access and preventing the sale of the foreshore and seabed, yet recognising ownership rights and interests. These could include the right to determine who uses the coastal area and for what, and commercial development rights.

The changing response of Government to the Court of Appeal decision

At first the policy was that the ownership of foreshore and seabed lies with the Crown. Then this became ownership that 'will be in the public domain' with general rights of access and not subject to private rights of ownership. Crown policy is that petroleum, gold, silver and uranium are owned by the Crown regardless of who owns the foreshore or seabed. Some recognition of customary rights as defined by the Maori Land Court was suggested, but with land below high-tide mark in the public domain to ensure public access. Few commercial rights would flow from these customary rights. Strengthened recognition of Maori interests in legislation, such as the Resource Management Act, could also provide economic spin-offs.

After a series of 11 hui around the country, where Maori opposition to the proposals was clearly expressed, the Government put forward a definite proposal.

Main points of the Government proposal (December 2003)

- **Principle of Access** — the foreshore and seabed should be public domain, with open access and use for all New Zealanders (some is already in private ownership).

- **Principle of Regulation** — the Crown to be responsible for regulating the use on behalf of all present and future generations of New Zealanders.

- **Principle of Protection** — processes should exist to enable the customary interests of whanau, hapu and iwi in the foreshore and seabed to be acknowledged and specific rights to be identified and protected.

- **Principle of Certainty** — there should be certainty for those who use and administer the foreshore and seabed about the range of rights that are relevant to their actions.

What this means to the seabed and foreshore

- The Government extinguishes the Maori right to seek private title to the foreshore and seabed.

- The ownership of the foreshore and seabed will be vested in the people of New Zealand, to be held in perpetuity, not able to be sold or disposed of except by Act of Parliament.

- The Maori Land Court can award customary title which recognises ancestral links to an area but public access remains protected.

- Sixteen regional groups involving Maori, local and central government will be set up to reach agreement on Maori participation in management of coastal activity.

- Redress will be possible if the court says customary rights are not adequately protected.
- A veto on Resource Management consents if the proposed activity impacts badly on customary rights.
- Development rights will not be part of customary rights unless they are a feature of a customary practice. However, title-holders can veto proposed developments that significantly restrict their ability to carry out a customary right.

Reactions to Government proposals — a range of views

A 21st-century confiscation

Te Ope Mana a Tai Chairman Matiu Rei said the proposal amounted to 'nothing less than a 21st century confiscation'. The Government was telling iwi and hapu they stood to lose little because there would have been few pieces of the coast where a private title would have been granted by the court. Mr Rei didn't agree. Te Ope Mana a Tai wants it left to the court to determine the rights.

Tu Wylie, a member of Te Ope Mana a Tai, said the Fijian Government should be congratulated on its transfer of ownership of coastal areas from the state to the indigenous Fijian tribes. He said New Zealand leaders lacked the courage and vision to take a similar step which would break the cycle of dependency.

A compromise settlement

John Tamihere says:

> We will not satisfy the screaming meemees at either end of this debate.

Another MP describes the policy as

> coming up with the best for Maori that middle New Zealand can stomach.

Too much given to Maori

National Party Reaction (December 2003): Dr Brash describes the policy as hitching

> another set of wagons to a Treaty of Waitangi gravy train that is out of control. The winners will be lawyers, bureaucrats and small sections of the Maori high-income aristocracy.

National is backing the policy that ownership lies with the Crown.

Waitangi Tribunal comments on the Government proposal

In February 2004 the Waitangi Tribunal reported on its hearing into the Government's foreshore and seabed proposals. It had to decide whether the proposals were consistent with the Principles of the Treaty of Waitangi.

The Tribunal could not agree with the Crown that the policy would benefit Maori. Rather, they found that the policy would take away Maori rights in exchange for participation in an administrative process from which they could possibly gain nothing. Maori would lose the right to go to the High Court and the Maori Land Court for definition and declaration of their legal rights in the foreshore and seabed. The policy therefore removed property rights and amounted to expropriation without a guarantee of compensation.

The recommendations of the Waitangi Tribunal

The tribunal gave the government six options:

- Start the process again and explore the options properly;
- Do nothing and leave it to the courts to decide;

- Provide for access and inalienability (Maori are aware of the anxiety about access and most do not want exclusive possession. There is room to manoeuvre);
- Improve the courts' toolkit so they can do a better job of the process;
- Use the Ngati Whatua — Orakei Reserves, Okahu Bay — example as a model which satisfies the Government's principles of access, regulation, protection and certainty without the need to vest legal ownership in either the Crown or the people of New Zealand and allows the mana of Ngati Whatua to stand tall. (Okahu Bay is managed between the Ngati Whatua and the Auckland City Council under the Orakei Reserves Act);
- Be consistent. The Tribunal noted that the Government was prepared to recognise the ownership interest of Ngati Tuwharetoa and of Te Arawa in the beds of their lakes and yet not prepared to vest any kind of title in the foreshore and seabed.

Government reaction to the Waitangi Tribunal recommendations

They didn't like it. Deputy Prime Minister Michael Cullen said it implied a rejection of Parliamentary sovereignty:

> The power of Parliament to change the law is central to the exercise of sovereignty . . .

Dr Cullen added that the Government does indeed recognise customary rights as a form of property rights.

About-turn in late February/March 2004

After National Party leader Don Brash made a speech attacking policies which he alleged favoured Maori on the basis of race, newspaper coverage criticising political correctness and pro-Maori policies, and National's sudden rise in the opinion polls, the Labour Government backtracked. Crown ownership was again on the agenda.

The New Zealand Herald, 8 March, 2004

The form of legislation proposed in April 2004

- It prevents the Maori Land Court awarding private title.

- Ownership of the foreshore and seabed is vested in the Crown.

- The Maori Land Court can register groups' ancestral connection with particular coastal areas if they have had a connection with the area since at least 1840.

- Maori groups can approach the Government directly to negotiate agreements for 'ancestral connection'.

- The Maori Land Court can register customary rights of groups that have carried on a particular activity in an area largely uninterrupted since 1840.

- Groups with ancestral connections or customary rights have greater rights in decision-making with local government bodies under the Resource Management Act and Conservation Act, and in some cases a veto.
- It abolishes the right of Maori to claim customary (aboriginal) title under the High Court common-law jurisdiction.
- It renames 'customary title' as 'territorial customary rights' and allows for compensation if the High Court finds that claimants would have been awarded customary title were it not for this legislation.

Te Ope Mana a Tai
The Bill confirms the worst fears of Maori. The findings and recommendations of the Waitangi Tribunal have been ignored or selectively applied. A number of new restrictions have emerged, such as a time limit on applications for recognition of ancestral connection and customary rights (December 2015), and no provision for legal aid.

The view of the National Party
It still gives far too much to Maori in the opinion of Don Brash. The National Party believes the proposal will give Maori dual management over almost the whole coastline and too much power to extract koha (compensatory 'gift') over resource management applications.

Where we are at the moment (late May 2004)
Possible abstention from voting for government legislation by Maori MPs
The Foreshore and Seabed Bill has passed its first reading in Parliament (there are three readings before it becomes law), with New Zealand First votes compensating for the lack of

support from some of the Maori Labour members. Nanaia Mahuta (Tainui) abstained, while Tariana Turia, having resigned from the Labour ranks in opposition to the legislation, faces a by-election and is promising to form a new Maori political party. The hikoi (march) to Parliament of some 20,000 people, which protested vehemently against the legislation, provided some indication of strong support for such a move. Meanwhile, the public has been invited to present submissions on the proposed legislation before 12 July 2004.

Key Points

- These potential property rights come from customary rights, not the Treaty of Waitangi.

- New Zealand law has not defined customary rights clearly.

- The new law (2004) will prevent Maori from going to Court to see if they can get freehold tenure to seabed and foreshore.

- Ownership will be vested in the Crown with some small concessions to Maori customary rights.

- There has been strong Maori opposition to the loss of their rights. Are we creating a new round of grievances?

Further Reading

Website of Te Ope Mana a Tai: www.teope.co.nz

Government website: www.knowledge-basket.co.nz

National Party website: www.national.org.nz

New Zealand First website: www.nzfirst.org.nz

Labour Party website: www.labour.org.nz

Chapter 12

Some Common Questions

What are iwi and how are they organised?

Traditionally, iwi were loosely organised networks of hapu. Some tribes were organised around the Maori Trust Boards established under the Maori Trust Boards Act 1955, mostly to receive and distribute compensatory payments from government for various injustices. Other iwi had no clear tribal structure apart from customary networks and informal alliances between hapu. In some areas District Maori Councils were like iwi structures but were regional rather than tribal.

But the Crown needed to be sure iwi were properly organised and could deliver government programmes efficiently. New policies required government agencies to consult with iwi, form partnerships with them and hand over services and resources to them. Government had to know who to approach, and which of several organisations could speak for the tribe as a whole. For example, a new programme instituted in 1986, called Matua Whanau, for the care of difficult children, arose from Maori initiatives and involved the whanau placing the child rather than the Department of Social Welfare.

Ngati Porou was one of the first to adopt a new structure in 1987, forming Te Runanga o Ngati Porou. Several other iwi followed. Many opted to retain existing trust boards. Others formed incorporated societies for the same purpose. Ngai Tahu has created a new structure — Te Runanga o Ngai Tahu —

accountable to Ngai Tahu and providing a body to represent the tribe in dealings with Crown and local government. There was some opposition from those who felt the rights of hapu would be undermined. Tainui and Whakatohea are undertaking the same consultation process.

The Office of Treaty Settlements encouraged this move. Tribes negotiating Treaty claims were expected to demonstrate that they had a mandate before signing, and an appropriate infrastructure to manage settlement packages. For iwi like Tainui, Whakatohea and Ngai Tahu, negotiations were handled by tribal trust boards. But trust boards were appointed by the Minister of Maori Affairs, were accountable to the Crown not to the tribe itself, and therefore not suitable for governing the tribes' assets.

Te Ohu Kai Moana developed criteria for iwi status such as recognition by neighbouring iwi, having a network of marae and hapu, and descent from a common ancestor. Tribal organisations needed to show that they had been elected at an advertised hui, had a constitution which allowed members to participate in decision-making, and had an executive which represented all the membership.

In addition to the traditional iwi there are also urban-organised iwi, like Te Whanau o Waipareira and the Manukau Urban Authority who played a significant role in the fisheries debate. There are also church-based groups, councils, committees, educational trusts and urban authorities — all reflecting the diversity of Maori society and its changes in aspirations.

What is meant by Tino Rangatiratanga?

It is the right of Maori to determine their own policies, to actively participate in the development and interpretation of the law, to assume responsibility for their own affairs and to plan for the needs of future generations.

Maori development depends on economic self-sufficiency.

This means Maori ownership and management of Maori resources, the use and development of te reo Maori and full Maori participation in the economy. In education, it means Maori programmes for Maori and by Maori. For problems which are significant to Maori, it means Maori solutions using Maori methods.

What is the legal definition of Maori?

What is measured today draws heavily on the census; Maori have been included since 1858. The definition of Maori has changed from a definition based on degrees of blood and mode of living to ethnic affiliation, descent or ancestry, regardless of degree.

Before 1926 the census definition of Maori was: 'persons of more than half Maori blood and Maori European half-caste living as Maori' i.e. as members of tribes; half-castes not living as Maori were classified as Europeans. Between 1926 and 1971, the mode of living portion was dropped. The definition became 'persons of half or more of Maori blood'. In 1986 the emphasis moved away from degree of blood to ethnic affiliation and in the 1991 census there were three definitions:

- NZ Maori ethnic — as one of their ethnic origins;
- Maori — as only ethnic origin;
- Do you have any Maori ancestry? — state iwi affiliations.

Ethnic identity for both Maori and Pakeha is in part a matter of personal choice, a subjective decision. To be Maori one needs at least one Maori ancestor and to identify with a particular tribe and family. Final confirmation of such identification rests with the other members of the kinship group, but the personal commitment is the central prerequisite. For many Maori their commitment and tribal identity is continuous and beyond question. Others make a definite decision to change from one culture to another, or simply drift in or out. Yet others may want to identify with more than one ethnic group. Flexibility and intermarriage are essential lubricants of an ethnically tolerant society. Both help in keeping the gap between cultures from becoming too sharply defined and too wide.

Why do Maori have separate seats in Parliament?

In 1867 four separate seats were created for Maori voters, motivated in part by the need to balance representation between the North and South Islands. The decision was based on neither the Treaty of Waitangi nor principles of fair representation. In terms of population, Maori were entitled to many more seats. There are arguments for and against continuing the separate seats but the strongest argument in favour of retaining them is the support Maori give to a separate voice in Parliament. When Maori consider the seats no longer necessary they will all register on the general roll.

Since 1975, Maori have had the option to register on either the Maori or general roll but have to stick with that for five years until the next census. With the introduction of MMP came the chance to increase the number of Maori seats. If all Maori had taken up the chance to enrol on the Maori roll, some 12 or more Maori seats would have been possible. Between February and April 1994 the option was open. After a claim was made to the Waitangi Tribunal, it agreed that the Crown had not put enough resources into informing Maori of their options. The Government rejected the recommendation. Some 1323 Maori were enrolled on the Maori roll and only one extra seat confirmed. The total number increased from four to five.

Not all Maori wanted to increase the Maori seats. The option was opened again in 1997 and more generously funded. The 1996 General Election saw more Maori candidates in a wider range of parties than ever before, plus a new Maori seat. Maori were affiliated to a wide range of mainstream parties. There were about 88 Maori candidates in electorates or lists and all the Maori seats were captured by NZ First. There were 15 Maori MPs in Parliament.

In 2004 there are seven Maori seats. The seats are Te Tai Tokerau (the old Northern Maori) Te Tai Hauauru (Western), Te Tai Rawhiti (Eastern), Te Tai Tonga (Southern), Tainui, Tamaki Makaurau, and Waiariki. Maori voters on the Maori roll equal those on the general roll.

Some questions about Waitangi Tribunal claims

Haven't there been claims before this?

There were a number of attempts in the past to settle grievances but they did not look at all their aspects. It is only in the last few years that the courts have spelt out the principles of the Treaty now used in the settlement process.

Are settlements final?

Yes, claimants cannot bring up their claims again before the Tribunal or the courts once a settlement has been reached.

Is private land available for use in Treaty settlements?

Since 1993 private land has not been available. However, if there is a willing seller or if the land had a compulsory acquisition order on it when the private owner bought it, an exception would be made.

Can conservation land be used in settlements?

Generally conservation land is not available. But specific sites of special significance may be transferred to claimants. These may have special conditions attached about public access or environmental values.

Why isn't there a time limit on claims?

It is important to get it right this time. The Crown wants to address all claims as soon as possible, but cannot force claimants to begin negotiations. A specific cut-off date would too rigidly confine the process and might mean that well-founded claims were not dealt with. Anyway, there is a limit to the number of claims that the Crown can deal with at any one time.

Why are Waitangi Tribunal discussions held on marae?

Decisions made on a marae carry more weight, and the agenda is controlled by the tangata whenua, so it is the preferred venue for an important hui.

What does it mean?

A marae is a traditional meeting place for formal and informal debates and decisions. Most ancestral marae are found within the tribal area. They can have origins dating back decades or even centuries. A marae reflects the culture and history of its members, their shared ancestors, common journeys, joint fortunes and misfortunes. Most marae centre on whanau or hapu; no two are the same. New marae have been established (sometimes in urban areas) to meet the needs of Maori living in the area, regardless of tribal origin. Marae operate like a community facility. They are governed by trustees who represent the whanau, and they maintain their independence from outside interference very strongly, but they do have to conform to local by-laws and the Resource Management Act. They are also expected to conform to the custom of a particular tribe.

Is there special legislation favouring Maori?

Both National and Labour governments have set up programmes to assist Maori economic, social and educational programmes. The National Government in 1993 set up Te Mangai Paho as a Crown entity to recognise the Crown's responsibilities regarding the Maori language and Maori culture. Educational scholarships for tertiary assistance, special funding for schools with a high Maori and Pacific Island population, and training programmes for employment have been created. The Labour Government initiated a health programme specifically to reduce Maori smoking.

Do customary fishing rights give Maori special privileges?

Yes, but it applies only to the specific tribe or hapu for that area. These are property rights originating from the customary rights and aboriginal title of indigenous people. They do not conflict with the general principle of equality under the law; for example, muttonbird harvesting from the Crown-owned Titi Island is only for Rakiura of Ngai Tahu and only for Ngati Wai from the Mokohinau Islands. Ngati Tuwharetoa alone are allowed to fish for koura (freshwater crayfish) and whitebait in Lake Taupo. These rights are held by local iwi or hapu and exclude other Maori and all non-Maori. They have possessed these rights for generations.

There are also special camping rights (nohoanga) for a fixed period of time each year on an area of Crown-owned land near a lake, river or other source of customary food. These reflect the ancient practices of seasonal fishing or food gathering.

Further Reading

'Healing the Past, Building a Future — A guide to Treaty of Waitangi claims and direct negotiations with the Crown', Office of Treaty Settlements

www.treatyofwaitangi.govt.nz

Further Reading

'Healing the Past, Building a Future — A guide to Treaty of Waitangi claims and direct negotiations with the Crown', Office of Treaty Settlements, October 1999.

Asher, George and Naulls, David, 'Maori Land', Planning Paper No. 29, March 1987, New Zealand Planning Council, Wellington.

Ballara, Angela, *Iwi: the Dynamics of Maori Tribal Organisation from c.1769–c.1945*, Victoria University Press, 1998.

Belich, James, *Making Peoples: A history of the New Zealanders from Polynesian settlement to the end of the Nineteenth Century*, Allen Lane for The Penguin Press, 1996; Penguin paperback edition, 2001.

Binney, Judith, 'The Maori and the signing of the Treaty of Waitangi' in *Towards 1990: Seven leading historians examine significant aspects of New Zealand history*, ed. David Green, Government Printing Office, 1989.

Durie, Mason, *Te Mana, Te Kawanatanga: The Politics of Maori Self-Determination*, Oxford University Press, 1998.

Graham, Douglas, *Trick or Treaty?*, Institute of Policy Studies, Victoria University, 1997.

Green, David, ed., *Towards 1990: Seven leading historians examine significant aspects of New Zealand history*, Government Printing Office, 1989.

Howe, Kerry, *The Quest For Origins: Who first discovered and settled New Zealand and the Pacific Islands?*, Penguin Books, 2003.
King, Michael, *Nga Iwi o Te Motu: 1000 years of Maori history*, Reed, 1997.

McHugh, Paul, 'A History of Crown Sovereignty in New Zealand', in *Histories, Power and Loss: Uses of the Past — A New Zealand Commentary*, eds. Andrew Sharpe and Paul McHugh, Bridget Williams Books, 2001.

Mulgan, Richard, *Maori, Pakeha and Democracy*, Oxford University Press, 1989.

Orange, Claudia, *The Treaty of Waitangi*, Allen & Unwin, Port Nicholson Press, 1987; new edition Bridget Williams Books, 1994.

Renwick, William, *The Treaty Now*, GP Publications, 1990.

Salmond, Ann, *Two Worlds: First Meetings of Maori and Europeans 1642–1772*, Penguin Books, 1991.

Sharp, Andrew and McHugh, Paul, eds., *Histories, Power and Loss: Uses of the Past — a New Zealand Commentary*, Bridget Williams Books, 2001.

Ward, Alan, *An Unsettled History: Treaty Claims in New Zealand Today*, Bridget Williams Books, 1999.

Williams, David V., *'Te Kooti tango whenua': The Native Land Court 1864–1909*, Huia Publishers, 1999.

Websites

www.treatyofwaitangi.govt.nz

www.waitangi-tribunal.govt.nz

www.teope.co.nz — Te Ope Mana a Tai

www.tokm.co.nz — Te Ohu Kai Moana: The Treaty of Waitangi Fisheries Commission

www.labour.org.nz — Labour Party

www.national.org.nz — National Party

www.nzfirst.org.nz — New Zealand First

Illustration Credits

Text illustrations: Holly Roach

Map on page 35 based on tribal location map in *Nga Iwi o te Motu* (Michael King, Reed, 1997)

Image on page 39: Alexander Turnbull Library, PUBL-0151-2-013

Map on page 71 based on Raupatu map in *A Century of Change* (Marcia Stenson and Erik Olssen, Longman, 1997)

Maps on page 77 by Max Oulton, published in *Waitangi Tribunal National Overview* (Alan Ward, GP Publications, 1997)

Cartoon on page 82 by Peter Bromhead

Map on page 103 based on Muriwhenua map in Muriwhenua Land Report (Waitangi Tribunal, 1997)

Diagram on page 131 based on coastal marine area diagram in *Healing the Past, Building a Future* (Office of Treaty Settlements, 1999)

Cartoon on page 141 was published in The New Zealand Herald, 8 March 2004, and appears courtesy of Rod Emmerson and *The New Zealand Herald*